STEVART

D0175348

SACAGAWEA

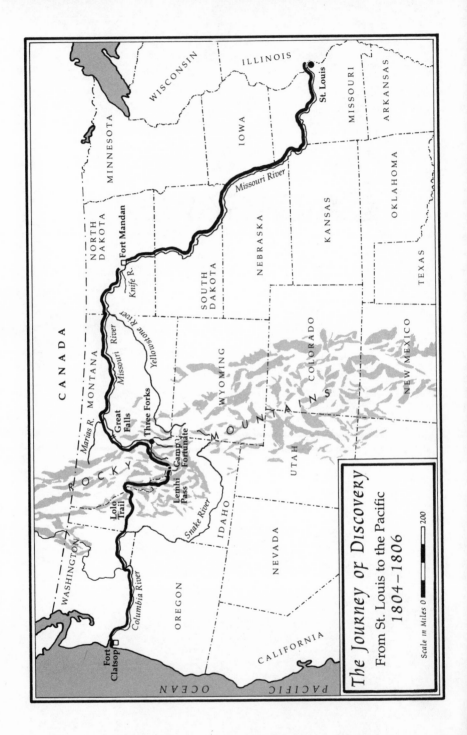

The Journey of Discovery
From St. Louis to the Pacific
1804–1806

Scale in Miles 0   200

Sacagawea

Judith St. George

G. P. Putnam's Sons   New York

G. P. Putnam's Sons, a division of Penguin Putnam books for
Young Readers, 345 Hudson Street New York, NY 10014.
G. P. Putnam's Sons, Reg. U. S. Pat. & Tm. Off.
Published simultaneously in Canada.
Printed in the United States of America.
Designed by Gary Bernal.
Text set in Palatino.
Maps by Karen Savary.

Library of Congress Cataloging in Publication Data
St. George, Judith, 1931- Sacagawea/ Judith St. George p cm.
Includes bibliographical references and index.
Summary: Tells the story of the Shoshone Indian girl who served
as interpreter, peacemaker, and guide for the
Lewis and Clark Expedition to the Northwest in 1805-1806.
1. Sacagawea, 1786-1884—Juvenile literature. 2. Shoshone women—
Biography—Juvenile literature 3. Shoshone Indians—Biography—
Juvenile literature. 4. Lewis and Clark Expedition(1804-1806)—
Juvenile literature. [1. Sacagawea, 1786-1884. 2. Shoshone
Indians—Biography. 3. Indians of North America—Biography.
4. Women—Biography. 5. Lewis and Clark Expedition(1804-1806)]
I. Title. F592.7.S123S7 1997 978′.00497′0092—dc21 [B] 96-49311 CIP AC

ISBN 0-399-23161-7

9 10

To Theodore Howe,
with love

CONTENTS

INTRODUCTION   /ix

CHAPTER 1   War Party   /1

CHAPTER 2   Wings   /4

CHAPTER 3   Strangers   /8

CHAPTER 4   Winter Beginnings   /13

CHAPTER 5   Leave-Taking   /17

CHAPTER 6   A New Heroine   /23

CHAPTER 7   White Bears   /27

CHAPTER 8   A Hard Time   /32

CHAPTER 9   A Friend   /37

CHAPTER 10   Sunshine in the Heart   /41

CHAPTER 11   Jumping Fish and Cameahwait   /47

CHAPTER 12   Horse Traders   /51

CHAPTER 13   The Crossing   /55

CHAPTER 14   Roots and Fish   /59

CHAPTER 15   Whitewater   /62

CHAPTER 16   Faces Along the River   /66

CHAPTER 17   Point Distress   /71

CHAPTER 18   Generosity   /75

CHAPTER 19   Long, Wet and Boring   /79

CHAPTER 20   Upstream Terror   /85

CHAPTER 21   True Happiness   /89

CHAPTER 22   Lessons To Be Learned   /93

CHAPTER 23   Dangerous Decisions   /97

CHAPTER 24   A Sad Farewell   /103

EPILOGUE   /107

BIBLIOGRAPHY   /109

INDEX   /113

Introduction

IF IT HADN'T BEEN FOR President Thomas Jefferson, Sacagawea would have lived out her life in the wilderness as the unknown Shoshone wife of a French-Canadian fur trapper. Instead, Sacagawea has had more memorials dedicated to her than any other American woman—markers, mountain peaks, lakes, parks and a river. She has also been the subject of statues, paintings and music.

In 1803, the United States, under President Thomas Jefferson, bought the Louisiana Territory from France. The 838,000-square-mile area lay between the Mississippi River and the Continental Divide. Because foreign countries made claims on the land west of the divide, President Jefferson wanted to strengthen American ties there. He also wanted control of the profitable Indian fur trade.

To attain his goals, Jefferson appointed Captain Meriwether Lewis to find a water route to the Pacific Ocean. He told both Lewis and Lewis' co-commander, William

Clark, to keep a daily journal. On their Journey of Discovery they were to study and describe the natural world—animals, birds, reptiles, fish, plants, trees, minerals, rivers and mountains. They were to draw detailed maps. And they were to learn everything they could about the western Indian tribes.

Lewis, Clark and a corps of soldiers left St. Louis in May, 1804, and headed up the Missouri River. In October, they camped for the winter near the Minnetaree village where Sacagawea lived with her husband. (Minnetarees were also known as Hidatsas and Gros Ventres.) When the Corps of Discovery left in the spring, Sacagawea, her husband and infant son were with them.

Over the years, Sacagawea's name has been spelled Sakakawea and Sacajawea. Whatever the spelling, all that is known about her can be found in the journals of Lewis and Clark, in journals that several of the soldiers kept, and in letters that were written at a later time. They tell of Sacagawea's capture, her marriage, the birth of her son and the role that she played on the Journey of Discovery. Only slight references to her later life exist.

Sacagawea, like her Shoshone people, who were sometimes called Snakes, was quiet, rather shy, practical, resourceful and cheerful in times of trouble. Shoshone women were compassionate and affectionate with their families and held their friends in high esteem. Traditionally they also had a voice in tribal affairs.

Sacagawea's more than five-thousand-mile Journey of Discovery also became my journey of discovery. My husband, David, and I traveled from Fort Mandan up the Missouri River and along sections of the Yellowstone and Columbia rivers on the Lewis and Clark Trail. The trips that we took, and the research that I did, brought Sacagawea to life for me. Having come to know her, I have occasionally taken the liberty of assuming what her reactions and emotions would have been. As I wrote her story, Sacagawea became more than just the subject of a biography. She became someone I care about and admire. I shall always think of her with fondness.

CHAPTER 1

WAR PARTY

THE YOUNG SHOSHONE GIRL and her friend were picking berries when they saw a cloud of dust in the distance. Others in the Shoshone camp saw it, too. Right away the two girls knew what it was and so did everyone else. An enemy war party was galloping toward them. The girls dropped their rawhide sacks. The bright berries scattered as they started running.

Mothers snatched up their babies and called for their older children to hurry. Men raced for their horses. Dogs barked. The river, head for the river. It was their only chance of escape.

The young Shoshone girl, who was about eleven, was small and slender but she was fast. Her dark hair flew behind her as she and her friend raced down to the river. Everyone in the camp was running for the river, too. If they could make their way upstream, the enemy warriors might not find them.

The young girl plunged into the clear, cold water. She hugged the sandy shoreline as she tried to keep up with her friend who was already ahead of her. Although the river was shallow, smooth rocks made the riverbed slippery. The girl's moccasins filled with water and her wet deerskin leggings slowed her down. Even so, the women and other children lagged behind. Only her friend ran faster. And then she heard the terrifying shriek of Minnetaree war whoops.

The Minnetarees were a tall, bold and powerful people who lived on the Missouri River many hundreds of miles away. Although the Shoshones were small and not very strong, fear drove them on. The women and children ran from the Minnetarees—one mile, two miles, three miles, until they could go no farther. A grove of cottonwood trees grew beside the riverbank. They would hide there.

Although her friend had disappeared around a bend in the river, the girl kept going. Her chest was ready to explode but she couldn't stop. She knew that the Minnetarees were mounted and armed.

Behind her, she heard shots and screams. She stumbled and almost fell. The Minnetarees had found the women and children. If only she could keep up with her friend, but the current was strong against her. Staggering and breathless, she could run no farther. Her only hope was to crouch in the bushes on the other side of the river. She saw a sandbar where it was shallow enough to cross to safety.

But there was no safety. She was halfway across the river when two war-painted Minnetarees bore down on her, their horses splashing through the water. One warrior galloped past her and seized her friend. The other warrior, wearing only a breechcloth and moccasins, loomed above the young girl like a giant. And then her world turned topsy-turvy. A strong arm swept her up as easily as if she were a fish being plucked from the stream. Captured!

CHAPTER 2
WINGS

EARLY IN NOVEMBER, 1804, the young Shoshone woman and her husband returned to their Minnetaree village from a hunting trip. High overhead, birds were flying south for the winter: ducks, geese, swans, cormorants, pelicans, herons and thousands more.

The young woman looked up. Five years had passed since she had been brought here to the Missouri River as a Minnetaree slave. She sighed as she watched the birds' free flight. If only she had wings to fly back to her Rocky Mountain home more than five hundred miles away.

The Minnetarees had named their Shoshone captive Sacagawea, which meant Bird Woman. Because the Minnetarees believed that birds held sacred powers, it was a name of respect. Sacagawea, who was about sixteen, was married now and no longer a slave. Forty-six-year-old Toussaint Charbonneau, a French-Canadian

fur trapper and trader, had bartered with the Minnetarees for two Shoshone captives, Sacagawea and Otter
Woman. Because Charbonneau didn't speak Shoshone
and Sacagawea didn't speak French, they talked to each
other in Minnetaree.

Charbonneau wouldn't have been Sacagawea's
choice of a husband, but then what woman ever had a
choice? Sacagawea was six months pregnant now and
didn't feel like a Bird Woman at all. She felt heavy and
earthbound.

As soon as Sacagawea and Charbonneau arrived in
their Minnetaree village, they heard about the white
men who had come up the Missouri River by boat from
St. Louis. White men weren't that unusual. After all,
Sacagawea's husband was white, and white men often
arrived to trap or trade. But these white men were different. There were at least thirty of them and they were
soldiers.

Sacagawea and Charbonneau heard all about the two
soldier chiefs. After smoking the pipe of peace and giving out gifts, the soldier chiefs had told the Indians that
their Great Father, Thomas Jefferson, wanted all Indian
tribes to live in peace. He also promised that American
trading posts would soon bring needed goods to the Indians in exchange for furs and pelts.

The soldier chiefs added that the Great Father had

ordered them to find a water route all the way to the Pacific Ocean. They would camp here on the Missouri River for the winter and leave in the spring. In the meantime, they needed an interpreter who spoke Indian languages. When Charbonneau heard that, he decided he was the man for the job.

Sacagawea was bursting with curiosity, but Charbonneau wouldn't let her go with him to meet the soldier chiefs. This was a man's business. Sacagawea hardly ever argued with her hot-tempered husband and she didn't argue now. But she would find some way to see these soldiers for herself.

Charbonneau traveled from their village nine miles down to the white men's camp. The two chiefs introduced themselves, Captain Meriwether Lewis and Captain William Clark. As Charbonneau spoke French but very little English, one of the soldiers, who spoke both French and English, translated.

Charbonneau explained that he had lived most of his life in the wilderness. He knew the Minnetaree language like a native and sign language, too. He added that his two wives had been Shoshone captives and his youngest wife, Sacagawea, was a chieftain's daughter. Yes sir, he was just the man they were looking for.

Lewis and Clark agreed. There were two Mandan villages nearby on the Missouri River and three Minnetaree villages a little farther north on the Knife River. They had already hired René Jesseaume to be their Mandan interpreter. Now they needed a Minnetaree interpreter. Even better, Charbonneau's wives spoke Shoshone.

Lewis and Clark had hoped that they could travel the whole way to the Pacific by water. By now they feared that wasn't possible. They had heard that the Shoshones, who lived in the Rocky Mountains, owned many horse herds, and they would need horses to get over the Rocky Mountains. If one of Charbonneau's Shoshone wives came along, she could interpret when they bargained with the Shoshones for horses. They hired Charbonneau on the spot.

When Charbonneau returned home, Sacagawea couldn't wait to hear about the soldiers. As usual, Charbonneau was full of himself. He was going to be paid, and paid well, to go with the soldiers on what they called their Journey of Discovery. They would be the first white men to cross the continent and they would be passing right through Shoshone lands. The two captains wanted Sacagawea to come as their Shoshone interpreter.

Sacagawea was dumbfounded. Home! She was going home. She would see her family and friends and the towering mountains that she loved. Not only that, but she would also see the big sea, the Great Waters. She had been given wings after all.

CHAPTER 3

STRANGERS

SACAGAWEA COULD STAND THE SUSPENSE for only so long. A week after Charbonneau visited the soldiers, she and Otter Woman made their way down the Missouri River. They took four buffalo robes with them as gifts for the soldier chiefs.

What they found was noise and confusion. Twenty-five or thirty bearded white men were sawing, hammering and yelling at each other as they built a winter fort. Like the Minnetarees, Sacagawea lived in a large round lodge covered by sod. This soldiers' fort was a cluster of square log huts.

With curious Indians wandering around, no one paid attention to Sacagawea and Otter Woman. As Shoshones, they were both shorter and smaller than either the Minnetarees or Mandans. Besides, they were quiet and shy by nature.

Then one of the tall white chiefs happened to glance

their way. As he approached, Sacagawea saw that his hair and beard were red. She had never seen red hair before. It must be painted. As the redheaded chief was admiring their gift of the buffalo robes, Sacagawea noticed a tall, husky black man working nearby. Both Sacagawea and Otter Woman were copper-skinned, but this man was even darker. Sacagawea wondered what unknown tribe he came from.

What was even stranger was the huge, long-haired animal that looked like a small, shaggy black bear. He seemed to have free run of the camp and when he padded over and sniffed her, Sacagawea jumped back in alarm.

At that moment, Sacagawea wasn't sure she wanted to travel anywhere with these loud, bearded men and their frightening animal. Her baby was due in three months and she would never put her baby at risk.

A few days later, Charbonneau told Sacagawea and Otter Woman that Captain Lewis and Captain Clark wanted him to be handy to interpret for the Minnetarees. They were to move down by the soldiers' camp. Sacagawea wasn't happy, but she did as she was told.

Living near the white men's camp at least gave Sacagawea the chance to keep an eye on the Corps of Discovery, as the soldiers called themselves. The captains were as strange as their men. For some reason, they measured everything: the level of the river, the depth of the snow, the temperature of the air, the speed of the wind, the position of the stars. And then they wrote it all down.

On November 16, 1804, the soldiers moved into their fort even though it wasn't finished. The fort, which they named Fort Mandan, had two rows of huts, a storehouse, a smokehouse and a sentry box, all surrounded by an eighteen-foot-high fence.

Several weeks after the soldiers moved into Fort Mandan, Lewis and Clark told their interpreters, Charbonneau and Jesseaume, to move their families into the fort, too. They would each have their own hut.

Sacagawea found military life hard to get used to. She wasn't lazy, but she worked when she wanted, played when she wanted and did nothing if that was what she felt like. These men did everything together and all at the same time.

A bugle blew each morning to wake the soldiers up. Then they drilled and marched in double lines and had their guns inspected. They took turns standing guard. When the flag was raised in the morning, a cannon was fired. The first time the cannon went off, Sacagawea and Otter Woman clung to each other, sure that the world was coming to an end. Charbonneau laughed. If the Sioux attacked, that cannon would come in very handy, he told them.

Although Indians were allowed into the fort from dawn until dusk, on December 24, the soldiers announced that the next day was their Great Medicine Day. The gates would be closed to all Indians but the interpreters' wives.

Three volleys of gunfire on the Great Medicine Day woke Sacagawea with a start. The men were already awake, dressed and in a happy mood. They called out "Merry Christmas" to one another. They exchanged gifts. They cooked special food. The captains gave each man three glasses of rum.

After supper, the men square-danced. Sacagawea, Otter Woman and Jesseaume's Indian wife were fascinated. The men grabbed each other as partners and danced to the music of a tambourine, a bugle and Private Cruzatte's fiddle. They jigged, jogged, pranced, clapped their hands and stamped their feet. Despite his weight and size, the black man danced better than anyone else. Sacagawea laughed out loud at the soldier who danced on his hands.

As she watched the merrymaking, Sacagawea remembered how lonely she had been as a Minnetaree captive far from home. These men were lonely and far from home, too. They were just trying to make the best of it by giving one another gifts, feasting and dancing. That was what her people did when they celebrated a special day. Why, they weren't so different after all. She had been mistaken to think that her baby would be at risk. Come spring, she, her husband and their baby would head out with the soldiers on their long journey to the Great Waters.

CHAPTER 4

WINTER BEGINNINGS

LIVING IN FORT MANDAN was a time of new beginnings for Sacagawea. Although she had gotten used to being pregnant, it was her first baby and she didn't quite know what to expect.

Certainly getting used to the military routine was a new experience, too. And she had to learn to recognize one bearded look-alike soldier from another. The dark-skinned man wasn't from an unknown Indian tribe after all. He was Captain Clark's servant and his name was York, while the big black animal was Captain Lewis' one-hundred-and-fifty-pound Newfoundland dog, Seaman.

Sacagawea was grateful for the blazing fire in their family hut. It was the coldest winter in any of the old ones' memories. The river ice cracked and groaned. The cottonwood trees boomed like gunfire. Buffalo herds crossed the frozen Missouri River without breaking through.

As the winter cold deepened, the soldiers' food stores began to run low. The Mandans were happy to supply the fort with corn, cornmeal and meat from the hunt . . . for a price. In exchange for food, Captain Lewis, as the company's medical expert, treated the Indians for frostbite, boils, cuts, fevers and snowblindness.

The corps' blacksmith traded work for food, too. He made arrow points and repaired the Indians' hoes, rakes and hatchets. Sacagawea watched him make battleaxes and repair guns. It was very puzzling. The two captains said their Great Father wanted all the Indian tribes to live in peace. Yet their blacksmith was turning out weapons that were plainly used only for warfare.

Lewis and Clark spent most of the winter planning their trip. They would travel up the Missouri River, over the Rocky Mountains and down the Columbia River to the Pacific. With René Jesseaume interpreting, the Mandans told the captains about the country that lay ahead. They traced the course of rivers in the dirt floor, made mountains out of sand and drew maps on hides. They also described the Indian tribes they would meet along the way.

Although the Minnetarees had traveled farther west than the Mandans, they weren't helpful at all. And the captains needed information about the Rocky Mountains. They visited the Minnetaree chiefs, gave them gifts and shared a peace pipe. The flattery worked. Charbonneau interpreted as the Minnetarees told Lewis and Clark what they wanted to know. Sacagawea had lived in the Rocky Mountains. She could have answered all the captains' questions but they never asked her.

By February, Sacagawea had grown to be very much at home in Fort Mandan, almost too much at home. As the interpreter's wife, she was beginning to feel rather important. Lewis and Clark entertained visiting chiefs and she saw no reason why she and Otter Woman shouldn't entertain their friends, too.

Although the fort gates were closed at sunset, from time to time Sacagawea and Otter Woman opened the gates at night and invited their friends in. The get-togethers would last late, with the women sharing gossip, laughter and games. One February night, the sentry saw Sacagawea and Otter Woman unlatch the gates. As soon as Captain Lewis heard about their late-night visitors, he ended their fun by putting a lock on the gates.

Only a week later, on an eighteen-below-zero February 11, 1805, Sacagawea's fun was over in more ways than one. She was in labor. Although she hadn't expected to have a hard time, she did. By dusk, the baby still hadn't come. Suddenly, Sacagawea was no longer the important wife of the interpreter. She was a frightened young woman, far from home.

Although Charbonneau had returned the day before from a hunting trip, he wasn't any help. Instead, it was René Jesseaume who told Captain Lewis that a small portion of a rattlesnake rattle would quicken the birth.

Lewis happened to have a dried rattle in his medicine kit. Although he had no faith that it would work, he was willing to try. And Sacagawea was more than willing to try. Lewis broke up two rings of the rattle, stirred them in water and gave Sacagawea the mixture. Only ten minutes later, the baby's head appeared and then the whole squirming little body. It was a boy, a fine healthy boy.

Weak and tired, Sacagawea looked down at her son as he was placed in her arms. He was beautiful, with a pair of healthy lungs. Charbonneau was as proud as if he had given birth to the baby himself. He announced that he would name his son Jean Baptiste after his friend the fur trader Jean Baptiste Trudeau.

Sacagawea agreed. Her life with her child was just beginning and in time she would call him a name that suited him better. After all, he would be her dearest traveling companion in the months to come.

CHAPTER 5

LEAVE-TAKING

SACAGAWEA SPENT FEBRUARY AND MARCH getting to know her baby and learning to care for him. She nursed him, sang him to sleep and carried him everywhere on her back in his cradle bundle. To fashion his cradle bundle, Sacagawea folded buffalo calfskins fur side in and sewed them together to make a sack. She slipped her naked baby into the sack with his feet resting on a skin filled with warm sand. He was protected by cattail down which she changed when it became soiled.

Little Jean Baptiste soon had a new name. Captain Clark called him Pomp, and Pomp it was. He was growing quickly and his bright eyes took in the world from his mother's back. A smile at Pomp brought a smile in return. Although only one of the young soldiers was married, most of them had brothers and sisters and Pomp was a sunny reminder of home.

As Charbonneau continued to interpret Lewis and

Clark's meetings with the Minnetarees, he grew more
and more arrogant. In March, when the captains told
him that his duties on the trip would be the same as the
soldiers', he protested. He said that he wouldn't work
or stand guard and if any man annoyed him, he would
turn back with his family.

After living with Charbonneau for three months,
Lewis and Clark had come to know him. The Indians
knew him, too. They mocked him with names such as
Chief of the Little Village and Great Horse from Afar.
Now Charbonneau had tested the captains' patience to
the breaking point. They said that if he couldn't live by
their rules, then he needn't come. They would get along
without him.

Charbonneau was furious. He ordered Sacagawea
and Otter Woman to pack up. They were leaving Fort
Mandan. The captains had dismissed him for no reason.

By now Sacagawea realized that Lewis and Clark
were fair and reasonable men. She also knew her husband. The two captains wouldn't have dismissed him
if he hadn't deserved it. In the heat of anger, Charbonneau often shouted at Sacagawea, even hit her, and she
put up with it. But she wouldn't put up with his ruin-
ing her one chance for an adventure. He could go back
and apologize.

Sacagawea didn't stand up to Charbonneau often,
but when she did, he listened. Besides, he was be-

ginning to realize his mistake. Lewis and Clark obviously weren't going to change their minds and they had promised him good money, twenty-five dollars a month. Much as he hated to apologize, he sent them a message saying that he was sorry for his foolishness. He would do all the work that was asked of him if they would take him back.

They accepted happily. They didn't care one way or the other about Charbonneau, but they did care about Sacagawea. They would need Shoshone horses to cross the Rocky Mountains and Sacagawea was their link with the Shoshones.

At last the long, brutal winter was over. The ice on the Missouri River broke up with a roar. The meadowlark announced spring with a burst of song. Choking clouds of smoke rose from fires that the Indians set to encourage an early growth of grass for the buffalo.

Everyone at Fort Mandan was at fever pitch to get started. But first the men had to load up their keelboat. On their sixteen-hundred-mile voyage from St. Louis, Lewis and Clark had drawn maps and written letters and reports. They had collected live birds and animals, hides, rocks, plants, animal skeletons, buffalo robes and Indian tools and weapons. Now seven soldiers, five boatmen and an Indian were taking everything back for the Great Father to study.

With the keelboat gone, the corps planned to travel

up the Missouri River in six dugout canoes and two pirogues. The flat-bottomed pirogues had square sails and smaller spritsails. Six oarsmen would row the white pirogue, while seven men would row the larger red pirogue. When the pirogues weren't being rowed or under sail, they were poled along, or towed from the shore by ropes.

Sacagawea was as eager to start as the soldiers. Long before they were ready to leave, she had packed clothes, bedding and supplies in her large, painted buffalo-skin case called a parfleche.

April 7, 1805, was the big day. Sacagawea dressed in her best. She wore deerskin leggings, ankle-high moccasins and a fringed garment of two deerskins sewn together, which was handsomely decorated with elk teeth. She wore bracelets, earrings, finger rings and a beautiful blue-beaded belt around her waist. She had braided her shiny black hair and painted the part red. As she carried Pomp in his cradle bundle down to the riverbank, she looked as small as a child herself.

The thirty-three members of the Corps of Discovery boarded the boats: Captain Meriwether Lewis, Captain William Clark, the French-Indian hunter and interpreter George Drouillard, Charbonneau, Sacagawea, Pomp, York, three sergeants and twenty-three privates. Last but not least was Lewis' Newfoundland dog, Seaman.

Both sides of the river were crowded with Minnetarees and Mandans who had come to see them off. Otter Woman was there, too, calling her farewells.

Although Sacagawea appeared calm as she stepped into the white pirogue with Pomp on her back, her dark eyes glowed. She would see her Shoshone people again. She would travel all the way to the Great Waters. She would have adventures that she couldn't even imagine. For five years, she had been flightless. Now she was going to fly. As the men pushed off from shore, Sacagawea's own Journey of Discovery had begun.

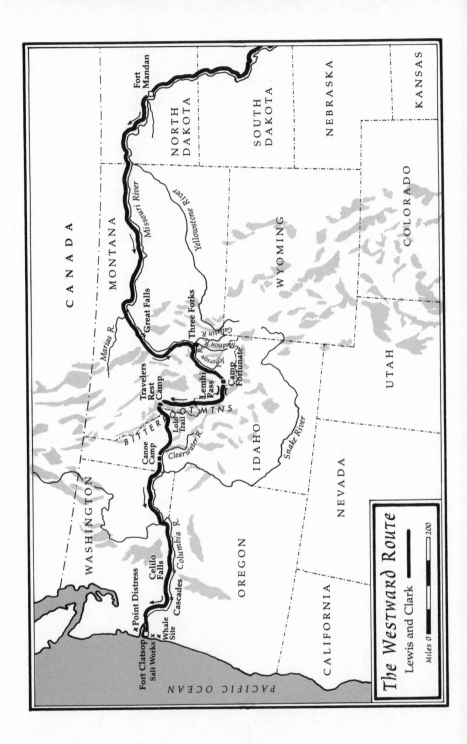

CHAPTER 6
A New Heroine

SACAGAWEA WAS PRACTICAL BY NATURE and from the very beginning, she was on the lookout for ways to help. When the corps camped for the night, she and York put up the buffalo-skin tipi that she slept in with Charbonneau, Pomp, Lewis, Clark and Drouillard. All the others camped in the open.

On the third day out, Sacagawea noticed a mound of loose dirt near some driftwood. She knew right away what it was. Poking in the dirt with a sharp stick, she found a large stockpile of white roots that a gopher had stored away. The roots were the size of a man's finger, and quite delicious. The men told her that they tasted just like Jerusalem artichokes.

Every time the corps stopped, Sacagawea searched for flavorful berries and roots. And she knew what she was doing. She was a Shoshone and for most of the year, Shoshones lived on wild plants, roots and fish.

With Pomp in his cradle bundle, Sacagawea picked baskets of redberries, serviceberries, gooseberries, chokecherries and purple currants. She dug up prairie turnips, small white onions and wild licorice.

Because game was plentiful, almost every meal was boiled, fried or roasted meat. Although the men especially liked buffalo tongues and beaver tails, their favorite was a buffalo sausage that Charbonneau cooked which he called *boudin blanc.* His finishing touch was to fry the sausage in bear oil.

An all-meat diet caused a disease called scurvy. Sacagawea had no way of knowing that fruits and vegetables prevented scurvy. Nevertheless, the berries and roots that she constantly gathered went a long way in keeping the men healthy.

Young as she was, Sacagawea also proved herself to be cool in a crisis. A few weeks into their journey up the Missouri River, she and Pomp were sitting under an awning in the white pirogue. Charbonneau, Cruzatte and four other men were also aboard, as were the captains' journals, instruments, papers, medicine kit, and trade goods which they planned to give to the Indians along the way.

Lewis called Charbonneau "the most timid waterman in the world." Only a short time before, he had been steersman when a strong gust of wind had almost overturned the pirogue. He had instantly panicked. Nevertheless, for some unknown reason, he was once again at the helm.

All of a sudden, a squall hit. The wind ripped the sail away from the man holding it and the pirogue tipped at a dangerous angle. Charbonneau again panicked. Instead of putting the boat into the wind, he luffed it broadside and it heeled over. Only the awning over Sacagawea and Pomp saved the pirogue from capsizing.

Sure that he was about to die, Charbonneau started screaming to God for mercy. Granted, he couldn't swim, but then neither could two other men on board. Although Sacagawea was a strong swimmer, Pomp was strapped in his cradle bundle on her back and she was as helpless as anyone else.

As the pirogue filled with water, Cruzatte yelled at Charbonneau to turn the boat into the wind. He was wasting his breath. Charbonneau was beyond hearing anything. Cruzatte pulled out his pistol and shouted that if Charbonneau didn't take hold of the rudder, he would shoot. The sight of the gun brought Charbonneau to his senses and he grabbed the rudder. Cruzatte then ordered two of the men to take down the sail and the other two to start bailing.

If anyone had reason to panic, it was Sacagawea, who

carried her darling Pomp in his cradle bundle. But she didn't. Barely able to balance herself in the stern of the boat that was already filled with water, Sacagawea first made sure that Pomp was safe. She then reached out and grabbed everything that was floating past her into the river. She had no idea what she was rescuing. All she knew was that the captains set great store by all these papers and equipment they had packed in watertight bags.

By the time Cruzatte and the other men were able to row to shore, the pirogue was barely above water. Although Cruzatte's quick thinking may have saved them from drowning, Sacagawea's quick thinking had saved what Lewis later said was worth his life. Until now Lewis hadn't paid much attention to Sacagawea one way or the other, but he praised her courage and cool-headedness. Sacagawea thought nothing of it. She had seen what needed to be done and did it. That was all.

Sacagawea couldn't speak English to the soldiers, or even French to her husband. But their journey had hardly gotten underway when she proved herself to be as valuable to Lewis and Clark as any man in the company.

CHAPTER 7

WHITE BEARS

LEWIS, CLARK AND EVERYBODY ELSE had grizzly bears on
their minds. The Minnetarees and Mandans, who called
them white bears because of their silver-tipped hairs,
hunted them only in parties of six or eight. Before start-
ing out, they painted and dressed as if going to war.

Grizzly bears were on Sacagawea's mind, too. She
didn't have to be told how fierce they were. She already
knew. She didn't have to be told what to do about them,
either. She had learned long ago to keep her distance.
Yet these foolish soldiers thought that because they had
superior guns, they could take on the white bears.

Sacagawea got in the habit of walking along the riverbanks with Clark and Charbonneau, carrying Pomp on
her back. She easily kept pace with the men. And the
walkers were able to stay even with the boats. Because
the boats were going against the current, they only
made about twenty miles a day.

Thirty-year-old Clark was good-natured and easy-going, and he and Sacagawea soon became friends. Although they had no common language, they pointed out objects or scenes of interest to each other. Clark solved the problem of Sacagawea's long and difficult name by calling her Janey.

As the party made its way up the Missouri River, they saw lots of bear tracks but no bears. Sacagawea was surprised that the men weren't alarmed by the size of the tracks. Clark measured one print that was almost a foot long.

The men may not have seen any bears, but because they ate hundreds of pounds of meat a day, they hunted constantly. When the two captains weren't hunting, they were studying and writing about the wildlife: buffalo by the thousands, deer, elk, pronghorn antelope, bighorn sheep, beaver, wolves, coyotes, moose, foxes, otters, porcupines, skunks and panthers, not to mention rattlesnakes. Hardly a day passed that someone didn't spot a rattler. Although there were close calls, no one was ever bitten.

They saw birds beyond counting: bald eagles, hawks, whooping cranes, swans, geese, ducks, woodpeckers, goldfinches, thrushes, robins, blackbirds, plovers, wrens and birds that neither Sacagawea nor anyone else recognized. Mosquitoes, ticks, fleas, gnats and blowflies were just as plentiful but a lot more annoying.

Seaman had his own wildlife experience. One day he swam after a wounded beaver that bit him in the leg. Lewis couldn't stop the bleeding and it was touch-and-go as to whether the dog would survive. (He did.)

Because the Great Father had ordered Lewis and Clark to write down everything they learned along the way, the captains carefully studied their surroundings. They then described what they had seen in their journals, sometimes even drawing pictures.

After weeks of travel, Lewis and a hunting companion finally met up with two grizzlies. They both fired, each hitting a bear. Although one wounded bear ran away, the other bear charged Lewis. But its wound slowed it down and the men had time to reload and kill it. It was a young male, weighing about three hundred pounds. He was no more dangerous than eastern black bears, the men all agreed.

Sacagawea didn't say anything. The Indians back at Fort Mandan had given fair warning. She just hoped that she and Pomp weren't around when the men encountered a full-grown adult.

Only a week later, Clark and Drouillard, who was the best hunter in the party, came on a large male grizzly. They fired and wounded him. He let out a fearful howl, plunged into the river and swam to a sandbar. He bellowed and roared for twenty minutes before dying. When the men dragged him to shore, Clark, as usual, did the measuring. The grizzly weighed about six hundred pounds, was more than eight feet long and had four-and-a-half-inch-long claws. And he had been hit by ten bullets.

The men were astonished by his size. They were even more astonished that he had lived so long with ten bullets in him. Although Sacagawea counted on the men having learned their lesson, they hadn't. The following week, one of the soldiers who had been walking on shore came running up to the boats. Breathless and terrified, he said that he had wounded a grizzly, which had pursued him for half a mile.

Lewis and seven men headed out to finish off the bear. They followed a trail of blood until they found it in thick brush. Despite its wounds, the bear had run for more than a mile and then had dug itself a deep pit and lain down. Lewis and the men shot it in the head and killed it. They were at last beginning to realize that the only way to stop one of these animals was a bullet through the head or heart.

A few days later, six men in canoes spotted a male grizzly and decided to go after him. Sacagawea watched them land their canoes and start out. Like her Shoshone people, Sacagawea was a gambler by nature and she knew that even six armed men weren't very good odds against one adult grizzly.

Approaching the bear, four of the men fired. All four bullets found their mark, with two bullets hitting the bear's lungs. Enraged, the grizzly charged. Two men shot again. One bullet broke the bear's shoulder and the other ripped into a muscle. The wounds only maddened him further and he took off after the men.

Two of the men slid down the riverbank and into their canoe. The other four scattered into a grove of willows. They fired again. Although two bullets struck the bear, he charged again. Two soldiers ran for the riverbank, leapt twenty feet into the water and began swimming. Despite having eight bullets in him, the bear jumped off the cliff and started swimming after the men. He was only a few feet behind them when one of the soldiers on shore killed him with a shot through the head.

What a terrifying experience! Much to Sacagawea's relief, the men's enthusiasm for grizzly bears dimmed. From then on, they treated grizzlies as she did, with the greatest respect . . . and at a distance.

CHAPTER 8

A HARD TIME

RIGHT FROM THE START, Lewis and Clark gave names to all the rivers and creeks that flowed into the Missouri River. Sacagawea found it strange. Most of the rivers and streams already had Indian names. But she was pleased when they called a river Charbonneau Creek and she was even more pleased when they named a lovely stream Sacagawea River.

Traveling up the Missouri, the company came to a magnificent river called the Yellowstone River. To celebrate the joining of two great rivers, each man was given a shot of whiskey. That evening Cruzatte brought out his fiddle and the men danced. Sacagawea always enjoyed both the music and the square dancing.

Five weeks later, on June 2, 1805, Lewis and Clark were surprised to arrive at a fork in the river. Although one fork was the Missouri and the other was unknown, they didn't know which was which. If they took the wrong fork, the whole expedition could fail. Sacagawea, who had never been this far north before, couldn't help. The captains would have to explore both forks and come to a decision.

Everyone needed a rest anyway. It had been raining for days. Swarms of mosquitoes and gnats made their life miserable. Game was scarce and the water was muddy. Many of the men were sick with colds, fevers, boils and dysentery.

After five days of exploring, Lewis and Clark agreed that the south fork was the Missouri River. And they were right. In honor of his cousin, Maria Wood, Lewis named the north fork Marias River.

Before they started out again, the captains had the men hide the red pirogue. To lighten their load, they buried gunpowder, dried food and supplies in a protected pit called a cache. They would pick everything up on their return trip.

On June 10, Lewis and four men went on ahead to find the Great Falls. Sacagawea didn't even notice they were gone. She was sick, really sick, with a fever, stomach pains and cramps. It was all she could do to nurse Pomp.

Clark did his best to doctor her. First he bled her by opening one of her veins with a medical knife called a lancet. Then he gave her a strong laxative. Sacagawea not only didn't get better, she got worse. Clark was worried, but he and Lewis had planned to meet at the Great Falls. They couldn't wait any longer to get started.

Although Sacagawea lay under an awning in the white pirogue, the next four days of travel were torture. She had never been a complainer, but now she groaned and cried out in pain. Nursing Pomp took every bit of strength she had. As Clark continued to bleed her and give her opium and laxatives, she grew weaker.

On June 15, Clark's party reached the magnificent Great Falls that crashed and thundered over five separate sets of falls. By this time, Sacagawea didn't know where she was, or care. She was near death and she knew it. Still, sick as she was, she sensed that Clark's bloodletting and medicines weren't helping and she refused any more treatment. Charbonneau, who had never been the most thoughtful of husbands, was finally alarmed. He told Clark that he wanted to take Sacagawea and his son back to their Minnetaree village. The idea was so foolish that Clark didn't bother to respond.

When Clark and Lewis were reunited the next day, Lewis was shocked at how sick Sacagawea was. She had been ill when he had left six days before, but now she was obviously dying. She had a high fever, a faint, uneven pulse, and her fingers and arms were twitching.

Lewis was nothing if not practical. Like Clark, he was

concerned about Sacagawea. But he was also concerned that if she died, they would have no one to interpret with the Shoshones for horses.

Lewis immediately gave Sacagawea two doses of Peruvian bark and opium for her fever, as well as mineral water from nearby sulphur springs. Because she trusted his medical skills, she took the medicine. By that night, her pulse was stronger and the pain had lessened. To help her sleep, Lewis gave her more Peruvian bark and opium.

In the morning, Sacagawea was better. Her fever had broken during the night and the pain was almost gone. For the first time in more than a week, she sat up. And she was hungry. A breakfast of buffalo meat and soup tasted good.

Only two days later, Sacagawea was well enough to take a walk with Charbonneau. They headed out onto the plains, where Sacagawea found the roots that the soldiers called white apples. She dug some up and ate them raw. When she returned to camp, she ate a large portion of dried fish. Right away, she was sick again with a fever and cramps. Lewis was furious. He had told Charbonneau exactly what Sacagawea was allowed to eat and Charbonneau hadn't listened.

Luckily, Sacagawea was young and strong, and in a day or two, she was better. All the men were relieved.

With her quiet, serene manner, it had been easy for them to take her for granted. But when they almost lost her, they realized how much she meant to them. She had gathered special roots and berries, mended their breeches and shirts and made them moccasins. But more than that, she and Pomp had brought a sense of loving family to lonely men far from home.

CHAPTER 9

A FRIEND

To celebrate feeling better, Sacagawea went fishing. The Great Falls were beautiful. The Missouri River tumbled down one magnificent waterfall after another into a series of whitewater rapids. But the falls presented problems. The men would have to transport their boats and all their baggage around the falls on foot. Because it was a steep eighteen-mile hike to the top of the falls, the less they had to carry the better. They hid the white pirogue in a grove of willows. Then they dug a pit and cached everything that they wouldn't need until their return trip.

To make their task easier, the men built two wooden wagon frames on which they loaded their canoes. But they faced almost impossible conditions as they carried or hauled everything around the falls. Prickly pear cactus cut their feet right through their moccasins. Violent rain- and hailstorms swept in from the west. Gnats and mosquitoes swarmed. Rattlesnakes lurked in the rocks and the grizzly bears were fiercer than any they had yet seen.

During the day Sacagawea and Pomp stayed close to their camp at the foot of the falls to avoid the grizzlies. Nighttimes were safer. Lewis' dog, Seaman, patrolled. If he smelled or saw a grizzly, he barked an alarm.

Sacagawea spent her days scraping, tanning and sewing skins. She was her usual helpful self. As the men brought in game from the hunt, she used the skins to patch shirts and breeches and stitch up dozens of new moccasins.

And then Sacagawea had her own frightening adventure. On June 29, she, Clark and Charbonneau left camp and headed out for the top of the falls. Sacagawea was carrying Pomp in a rawhide net sling instead of his cradle bundle. They hadn't gone far when they noticed a fast-moving black cloud. They would be soaked if they didn't find shelter. To wait out the storm, they dashed for a deep ravine protected by an overhanging rock ledge.

Strong winds brought the first burst of rain. That was followed by the most violent hail- and rainstorm that Sacagawea, or any of them, had ever seen. Hailstones hit the overhead ledge like cannonballs. Moments later, a flash flood came roaring down the ravine toward them.

They all reacted true to form. Charbonneau, who saved his own neck first, scrambled up the steep hill to safety. Sacagawea's immediate concern was Pomp. She grabbed him out of his sling and held him in her arms as she tried to get a foothold in the muddy hillside. As the last to leave, Clark pushed Sacagawea from behind. With the water already swirling around his waist, he shouted at Charbonneau to pull up Sacagawea from above.

Charbonneau either couldn't hear or was too frightened to act. Whichever, he was useless. Sacagawea had never been able to count on Charbonneau and she couldn't count on him now. Finally, through her own grit and determination and Clark's help, she made it up the muddy slope with Pomp.

By now the water in the ravine where they had been standing was fifteen feet deep. All their belongings were gone: the men's guns and equipment, Pomp's bedding and clothing, even the company's valuable compass. Although everyone was wet and cold, Clark was concerned mostly about Pomp and Sacagawea, especially Sacagawea, who had been so sick.

They ran all the way back to camp. Hailstones as big as apples covered the ground. Luckily, none of the men in camp was seriously hurt, but the hailstones had knocked some of them down. Others were bruised and bloody.

Although two men found the compass in the ravine the next day, everything else was gone. When Sacagawea heard how the ravine was filled with boulders, driftwood and mud, she knew that Clark had saved both Pomp's life and hers.

When she made an effort to find out how she could repay him, Clark brushed her thanks aside. He was fond of little Pomp, and Sacagawea was his friend, his good friend. Friends didn't have to be repaid. It was enough that they could be on hand to help each other out whenever help was needed.

CHAPTER 10

SUNSHINE IN THE HEART

CARRYING THE CANOES AND BAGGAGE around the Great Falls took eleven days of backbreaking effort. Finally, the company pushed off again into the Missouri River. Lewis and Clark had one goal: to find the Shoshones, bargain for horses and make it over the Rocky Mountains. Time was short. Except for six or seven weeks during the summer, the mountain passes were snowed in.

Sacagawea was eager to find the Shoshones, too. She could hardly wait to see her family and friends. Nevertheless, they had been traveling for more than three months and had yet to see any Indians.

And then, only four days after leaving the Great Falls, they found fallen-down wickiup shelters. They had come across abandoned Indian camps before, but they had never been Shoshone. These shelters, however, were the remains of a Shoshone camp. Sacagawea showed Lewis and Clark where the bark had been stripped off the pine trees. After a hard winter, her starving people peeled back the bark to eat both the tender underparts of the wood and the sap. She had done it herself.

By this time, the company was traveling in eight canoes. Lewis had brought a collapsible iron frame boat all the way from the East. Back at the Great Falls, Sacagawea had watched the men sew skins onto the frame. It didn't look watertight and it wasn't. Once launched, the boat had leaked hopelessly. The men had then had to spend five precious days making two more canoes.

After traveling through a gloomy six-mile-long canyon which Lewis called the Gates of the Rocky Mountains, they saw great clouds of billowing smoke in the distance. Sacagawea knew what it meant. A few days before, four soldiers had set off to look for the Shoshones. Instead of finding them, the search party had frightened them off. The Shoshones had set fires as a signal for their people to flee.

On July 22, Sacagawea recognized a stream that flowed into the Missouri River. Her people came down to this stream for the white face paint that lined its banks, she explained. Delighted that they were at last in Shoshone country, the captains named the stream White Earth Creek.

Not even Lewis and Clark were delighted for long. The corps ran into their longtime enemies: eye gnats, mosquitoes and prickly pear cactus. The gnats burrowed painfully under their eyelids, while mosquitoes swarmed in huge gray clouds that made even breathing difficult. The needle-sharp prickly pear cactus caused cuts, boils and infections. Seaman was in agony as the spines pierced his tender paws.

Three days later, the company reached Three Forks where three rivers came together to form the mighty Missouri. Lewis and Clark named the rivers the Jefferson, the Madison and the Gallatin after their president and his secretaries of state and treasury.

Reaching the headwaters of the Missouri River may have been a notable event for Lewis and Clark, but for Sacagawea, it was a place of dark and fearsome memories. She and her Shoshone people had been camping nearby when the Minnetarees had attacked. The Minnetarees had known that the Shoshones came down from the mountains to hunt buffalo in the fall. They had also known that the Shoshones had no guns to defend themselves. Badly outnumbered, the Shoshone warriors had mounted their horses and fled.

Sacagawea had always wondered what had happened to her friend. On their way back to the Missouri River, she had escaped their Minnetaree captors. More importantly, Sacagawea still didn't know the fate of her family. Most of the time, she could keep her fears at bay, but here, where it had all happened, they came flooding back.

After a two-day rest, the corps headed up the Jefferson River. They stopped for their noon dinner on the very spot where Sacagawea had been captured. She would never forget her terror as the Minnetaree warrior had scooped her out of the water. She couldn't leave this ghostly place soon enough.

For a week, the party continued up the Jefferson River. When the Jefferson branched, they took the left-hand fork, which was later known as the Beaverhead River. Once on the Beaverhead, Sacagawea saw another familiar landmark, a steep rock that the Shoshones called Beaver's Head because it resembled a swimming beaver. Sacagawea said they would meet up with her people soon.

This time she was wrong and they saw no one.

Thinking that a small party would have a better chance at finding the Shoshones, Lewis set off with three men, including Drouillard. But not Sacagawea. How strange. She had come all this way to interpret and Lewis had left her behind. Although Drouillard knew sign language, she was the only one who spoke Shoshone. And if she and Pomp were along, the shy

Shoshones would know that the men were peaceful, since a woman and child would never travel with a war party.

Lewis didn't hesitate to ask Sacagawea for advice before he left and she was gracious enough to give it. The closest Shoshone word for white man was "tab-babone," she told him. As a sign of friendship, he should wave a blanket in the air and then spread it on the ground. He should also paint the Shoshones' faces with vermilion paint as another sign of friendship.

Days passed, and Lewis and the three men didn't return. Tensions ran high. During one dinner, Charbonneau angrily slapped Sacagawea. Although her husband had hit her before, Clark had never seen him do it and he gave Charbonneau a tongue-lashing. Sacagawea was grateful. Clark had said he was her friend, and he was.

On the morning of August 17, 1805, Clark, Sacagawea, Pomp and Charbonneau were walking along the riverbank. Clark, who had painful boils on his ankle, lagged behind. Sacagawea and Charbonneau suddenly saw two men riding toward them. Their faces were painted and they both wore short ermine-skin capes. Her people! These were her people. Sacagawea danced up and down with joy.

Excited as she was, she didn't forget Clark. Turning

around so that he could see her, she raised two fingers to her lips, then swung her arm straight out in the sign language word for "friend" or "brother." Clark saw her. He understood. Painful ankle or not, he began to run.

Another sign language phrase expressed even better how Sacagawea felt. "Sunshine in the heart" said it all.

CHAPTER 11

JUMPING FISH AND CAMEAHWAIT

As the two riders approached, Sacagawea was surprised to see that one of the men was Drouillard. Dressed in a Shoshone cape, tan from the sun and with his face painted, he looked just like a Shoshone.

Drouillard explained that their party had found the Shoshones, all right, but the Shoshones had been frightened and had run away. Finally, they had been willing to meet with Lewis. After several days of communicating in sign language, Lewis had convinced the Shoshone chieftain to let Drouillard ride back to find Clark and the others. The chief agreed, but only if a Shoshone warrior rode with him.

If Sacagawea had been with Lewis, he wouldn't have had any trouble. Well, it hadn't been her decision to stay behind. Besides, right now all she cared about was seeing her people. Although she could have run the whole way, Clark's ankle still pained him. The least she could do was match her pace to his.

As they approached the camp, Sacagawea saw a crowd of Shoshones. Like a nest of stirred-up bees, they were buzzing around in a state of high excitement. How like her people. Now they were sure there was no danger, they were terribly curious. Sacagawea had come far from the days when she had never seen a white man, either. Here she was, married to a white man and traveling with white soldiers all the way to the Great Waters.

The Shoshones hadn't really believed Lewis when he had told them he was friendly. Now, seeing Sacagawea and Pomp, they saw it was true. In the middle of all the confusion, a young woman dashed up to Sacagawea and hugged her. Incredibly, it was her friend who had escaped from the Minnetarees.

Tears filled Sacagawea's eyes as she returned her friend's hug. They talked and cried and talked some more. Her friend proudly said that she was now called Jumping Fish from the way she had leapt through the water fleeing their captors. Neither young woman had thought she would ever see the other again. Yet here they were, both alive and well.

As soon as word spread that this young mother in Minnetaree dress was indeed a Shoshone, other women gathered around to greet her and admire little Pomp. Hearing the familiar soft words of praise and welcome in her own language was Sacagawea's true homecoming.

Despite her pleasure, it was hard not to notice how gaunt everyone looked. Hunger dulled their eyes and the children seemed especially thin and sad-faced. Sacagawea's heart went out to her starving people.

Late that afternoon, Sacagawea was told that the captains wanted her to interpret for them. They had built a tent of willow brush with a sailcloth awning for their meeting with the chief. When Sacagawea entered the tent, she saw Clark seated on a white robe with six pearl-like seashells tied in his red hair. The men had taken off their moccasins and the air was heavy with smoke from the peace pipes they had passed around.

Sacagawea had tried to prepare herself for the meeting. She knew that interpreting would be difficult. The chief would speak in Shoshone, Sacagawea would translate the Shoshone into Minnetaree, which Charbonneau would translate into French. One of the French-speaking soldiers would then translate the French into English for Lewis and Clark.

The chief spoke first. His voice sounded familiar. Startled, Sacagawea looked up. The chief was Cameahwait, her brother. With a cry, she jumped to her feet. She threw her arms around him, wrapped him in her blanket as a gesture of love and sobbed with joy. Cameahwait, who embraced his sister in return, had tears in his eyes, too. Everyone at the meeting was moved. After they exchanged a few words, Sacagawea sat down again. But she was overcome by emotion and she kept bursting into tears. At last, she was able to pull herself together long enough to interpret.

When the meeting was over, Sacagawea was finally able to ask Cameahwait about the rest of their family. She knew that someone must have died recently. Cameahwait's long hair was cut short as an expression of mourning. To her sorrow, he told her that they were all gone except for a brother who was off hunting and a sister's young son whom Sacagawea immediately adopted, at least in name.

Sacagawea meant Bird Woman, and like a bird, she had returned home. But the nest was nearly empty. She wept for her loved ones who had died. Still, she was grateful to have found her brothers and her nephew. For now that was enough.

CHAPTER 12

HORSE TRADERS

BEFORE THEY COULD BEGIN to trade for horses, Lewis and Clark had their men set up a camp on the Beaverhead River. They named it Camp Fortunate because of their good fortune in finding Cameahwait.

A middle-aged Shoshone man arrived at Camp Fortunate to talk to Sacagawea. When she was an infant, she had been promised to him as his bride, he told her. He had two wives and she would be his third. As soon as Sacagawea explained that she was already married and had a son, the man wasn't interested. That was fine with Sacagawea. She wasn't interested, either.

Lewis and sixteen men stayed behind at Camp Fortunate, while Clark headed for the main Shoshone village. Eleven soldiers, Sacagawea, Pomp, Charbonneau, Cameahwait and most of the Shoshones went with him. The village was forty miles away over a high mountain pass called Lemhi Pass. Clark and the eleven men were going to explore a possible river route, while Sacagawea and Charbonneau were to stay with the Shoshones. Although they had already traded some clothing and trinkets for three horses, Clark wanted Sacagawea to talk Cameahwait into returning to Camp Fortunate with more horses.

Clark trusted that Sacagawea would be successful and she was. A few days later, Sacagawea, Pomp and Charbonneau returned to Camp Fortunate with Cameahwait, some sixty Shoshones and best of all, a herd of horses. Lewis, who had been expecting them, handed out gifts to the chiefs and warriors in preparation for trading their horses.

Sacagawea didn't need to tell Lewis that the Shoshones were half-starved. He could see that. Lewis boiled some dried corn and beans that he had brought from Fort Mandan and served them to Cameahwait and his chiefs. Cameahwait told Lewis that the vegetables were the next-to-best food he had ever eaten. The best, he said, was a lump of sugar that Sacagawea had generously given him.

Lewis had his men close down Camp Fortunate. They packed up their supplies and sank all their canoes in the Beaverhead River to use on their return trip. And Lewis had Sacagawea interpret as he bargained with Cameahwait for horses. Although Lewis had never been Saca-

gawea's good friend the way Clark was, he respected
her. To show his appreciation, he gave Charbonneau
enough trade goods to buy a horse for Sacagawea. She
was delighted. Pomp was six months old now and
heavy to carry.

Early the following day, everyone in Camp Fortunate
began the trip back to the main Shoshone village. They
had just started when Sacagawea overheard Cameahwait make plans with his men to go buffalo hunting the
next morning. Sacagawea knew that if the Shoshones
left, the corps would be stranded in the mountains. Winter was closing in. Snow covered the nearby peaks and
ice coated the rivers. She told Charbonneau to let Lewis
know right away that Cameahwait and his men were
leaving to hunt buffalo.

But Charbonneau didn't report to Lewis until late
afternoon. Lewis was enraged. How long had Charbonneau known this? Charbonneau admitted that Sacagawea had told him early that morning. As far as Lewis
was concerned, it was the same old story. He and Clark
could rely on Sacagawea, but never on her dull-witted
husband.

Lewis talked to Cameahwait long and hard as Sacagawea interpreted. He said that Cameahwait had given
his word that he would see them safely over Lemhi
Pass. He had thought that Cameahwait was a man of

honor. Now Cameahwait was going back on his promise.

Cameahwait, in turn, explained that his people were starving. The women wept in despair for their hungry children. They couldn't wait any longer to hunt buffalo.

Sacagawea was caught in the middle. Her people were desperate, but Lewis and Clark were desperate, too. Finally, Cameahwait agreed to guide the company over Lemhi Pass before leaving for the hunt.

When they reached the main Shoshone village, there was a message from Clark. He confirmed what they had feared all along. There was no passable river route. Because they would have to cross the Rocky Mountains on horses, they would need twenty more mounts.

In the ten days since the white men had arrived, the Shoshones had learned a lot. They now wanted guns and ammunition for a horse, not just a few trinkets. When Clark rejoined Lewis and the others, he was surprised that a single horse cost him a pistol, a knife, gunpowder and ammunition.

In the end, the Shoshones traded twenty-nine horses and a mule. But when the corps picked up the horses, they found that some were very young, some were poor stock and most had weak backs. As horse traders, the Shoshones had won, hands down.

CHAPTER 13

THE CROSSING

THE CORPS OF DISCOVERY left the Shoshones on August 30, 1805. It was a day of decision for Sacagawea, whether to go with Lewis and Clark or stay with her people. Her Shoshone band would welcome her back. Pomp would be loved and petted. As Chief Cameahwait's sister, she would be held in high esteem.

But Sacagawea was a different person from the young girl who had left Fort Mandan four months before. She had earned her name, Bird Woman. She had been given wings and she didn't want to have those wings clipped now.

Sacagawea said her sad farewells knowing that she might never see Cameahwait or her people again. As she rode away, she kept looking back until her family and friends were out of sight. At least she was still able to speak Shoshone. A Shoshone, Old Toby, and his four sons were going to lead them over the mountains.

Three of Old Toby's sons soon turned back. Sacagawea couldn't blame them. First it rained, and then the
rain changed to sleet, which in turn changed to snow.
There was no game to be found. The trail led over sharp
lava rocks that cut the horses' feet. Everyone had to dis-
mount and walk.

After four miserable days, they came down into a
beautiful valley. Even better, the Indians who camped
there were friendly and shared what little food they
had. Lewis and Clark called them Flatheads, although
they weren't one of the tribes that flattened their heads.

A Shoshone boy lived with the Flatheads. With Sacagawea once again interpreting, Lewis and Clark bargained with the Flatheads for horses. They traded seven
of their scrawny horses for seven fine mounts and
bought thirteen more with trade goods.

Travel across the valley was pleasant. But the snow-
covered Bitterroot mountain range of the Rocky Mountains loomed in the distance. Lewis and Clark planned
to cross the Bitterroots on a buffalo road that was later
called the Lolo Trail. To rest up for the crossing, the
party camped for two days at a site they called Travelers Rest.

Rested or not, no one was prepared for what lay
ahead. It rained, hailed and snowed. The Lolo Trail
wound over rocky ridges, down deep ravines and

through heavy underbrush. Everyone gasped for breath in the thin mountain air. With no game to hunt, they killed, roasted and ate one of their colts . . . and named a nearby stream Colt-Killed Creek.

Sacagawea was as hungry as anyone else, but she was a Shoshone and Shoshones didn't eat horsemeat. It was important to keep up her strength to nurse Pomp, but she couldn't bring herself even to taste it. Half-starved, she began to question her decision. Perhaps it had been a mistake not to stay with her people. Risking her own life was one thing, but to risk Pomp's was another.

Each day brought a fainter trail and colder weather. Old Toby got lost and led them three miles out of the way. Several of the horses slipped and fell. The horse carrying Clark's desk rolled down a steep bank. Although the horse wasn't hurt, the desk was smashed. Writing had no meaning for Sacagawea, but she knew how Clark valued his notebooks and she helped pick up his scattered papers.

September 16 was the worst day of all. Everyone woke up wet and cold under a blanket of snow. Only Pomp, whom Sacagawea kept bundled snug in her robe, stayed dry. The men wrapped rags around their freezing feet and set out through a blizzard. On the two nights that followed, the men killed the last two colts.

Hungry as she was, Sacagawea still refused to eat horse-meat.

Desperate for food, Clark and six men went on ahead to hunt game. Their only find was an Indian horse that had wandered off. After eating a portion of their kill, they hung the rest from a tree. When Lewis and the men found the horsemeat that Clark had left for them, everyone but Sacagawea wolfed it down. Their party had eaten nothing for two days but a coyote, a crow, bear oil, dreadful-tasting portable soup, and candles.

On September 22, one of Clark's men met them on the Lolo Trail with a packhorse carrying food. He told them that his party had come out of the mountains onto the plains two days before. Indians in two villages had welcomed them, fed them and sent this food back. No news could have been more welcome to Lewis' starving company.

The Rocky Mountains had almost defeated the Corps of Discovery. Instead, the Corps of Discovery had defeated the Rocky Mountains. Sacagawea had wanted adventure. But the past eleven days on the Lolo Trail had been more of an adventure than even she could have wished for.

CHAPTER 14

ROOTS AND FISH

WHEN LEWIS AND HIS PARTY rode into the first Indian village, the women and children fled. They were sure that these strange white men were a war party. Only when they saw Sacagawea and Pomp did they return.

Because the Indians wore shells, rings and trinkets in their noses, they were called Nez Percés, which was French for "pierced noses." They lived on camas roots, dried fish and berries. Camas roots, which looked like onions, were eaten raw, boiled or pounded into powder to make soup, bread and puddings. Sacagawea was familiar with camas. Her Shoshone people lived on camas, too. She also knew enough not to eat great amounts at once.

The starving soldiers didn't know or care. They stuffed themselves with both camas bread and dried fish. They were faint with hunger. Furthermore, they had dropped down from the freezing, thin air of the mountains to the hot and humid plains. The change of climate, and especially the change of diet, was deadly.

The men became painfully sick with stomach cramps, diarrhea and vomiting. Lewis was sicker than anyone else. For days he couldn't even walk. Sacagawea, Old Toby and Old Toby's son were about the only ones who didn't fall sick. Unlike the soldiers, they had eaten camas all their lives, so their bodies were better able to digest it. And they hadn't overeaten.

Sick or not, the men had a job to do. A Nez Percé chief, Twisted Hair, drew a map on an elk skin and showed Clark their route. He said that Clark and his party would be able to travel by rivers the rest of the way to the Great Waters. But the corps had no boats. Before crossing the Lolo Trail, they had sunk all their canoes in the Beaverhead River. They would have to make new ones.

The company set out to find a stand of trees that would be large enough for canoe-making. The sick men were barely able to ride. Lewis couldn't even mount his horse without help. From time to time, they had to stop and lie down on the trail, doubled over with pain.

At last they found some good-sized pine trees on the Clearwater River. They stopped, set up a camp, which they called Canoe Camp, and began working. Although Clark gave the men medicine, it only made them sicker. Once again, Sacagawea came to the rescue. As the men began to cut down trees, she gathered special herbs and made salads, which helped to ease the men's bloating and gas pains.

The men worked on the canoes for the next ten days. Because they were weak and their axes were small, they burned out the tree trunks, Nez Percé style. They also branded their thirty-eight horses with Lewis' name. Chief Twisted Hair promised to see that the horses were taken care of until the corps returned and needed them to get back over the mountains. Although Lewis and Clark trusted the Nez Percés, they buried their saddles and ammunition secretly at night.

After two weeks of eating Nez Percé roots and fish, the Corps of Discovery was more than ready to leave. They pushed off into the Clearwater River on October 7, 1805, in their five new dugout canoes. It was a mixed crew: Lewis, Clark, twenty-six still-queasy soldiers, Sacagawea, Charbonneau, Pomp, Drouillard, York, Old Toby, Old Toby's son and Seaman. They may have been a mixed crew, but they were all in high spirits.

For four months they had paddled, poled and towed their boats upstream against the Missouri River current. Now that they were west of the Rocky Mountains, they would be going downstream with the current all the way to the Pacific. Surely, the worst was behind them.

CHAPTER 15

WHITEWATER

ALTHOUGH THE MEN HAD DONE THEIR BEST, they had been too weak and sick to make the canoes properly. One canoe was small and quite light, but the other four were large and awkward.

The Clearwater River was rough going and the corps ran into trouble right away. On their very first day, they hit ten sets of rapids. The canoe that Clark was riding in struck a rock and began to leak. Luckily, the men were able to repair it that night.

The next day wasn't any better. In fact, it was worse. When the company passed over fifteen more rapids, one of the canoes split open and sank. Those men who couldn't swim had to hold on to a rock for dear life until they could be rescued and their canoe towed to shore.

Whitewater canoeing wasn't for Old Toby and his son. They were mountain men, not rivermen. In the middle of the night, someone saw them running away. Lewis and Clark didn't understand why the two Shoshones hadn't asked for their pay. Sacagawea did. Anything of value they carried was sure to be stolen before they reached home.

It was hard to have them gone. Old Toby and his son were Sacagawea's last link with her band. Speaking Shoshone had given her great pleasure and she would miss hearing the familiar speech of her people.

Two Nez Percé chiefs, Twisted Hair and Tetoharsky, caught up with the corps to take over as guides. Twisted Hair had earlier promised to lead them and now he was keeping that promise. Like all Nez Percés, both men were strong swimmers and skilled rivermen. Although there was no common language between them, Drouillard and the two chiefs talked in sign language. Even Lewis and Clark had picked up sign language skills.

The banks of the Clearwater River were lined with Nez Percés fishing for salmon. Twisted Hair and Tetoharsky paddled their canoe ahead of the party. They explained to the Nez Percés that the white men who were coming were friendly and wanted only to trade.

Without saying a word, Sacagawea was even more of a help at easing their way. In spite of what the two chiefs told them, the frightened Nez Percé women and children ran and hid at the sight of the white men. But when they saw Sacagawea and Pomp, they knew that the Nez Percé chiefs had spoken the truth. Only then were they willing to trade their salmon and camas roots for trinkets and goods.

When the company arrived at the junction of the Clearwater and Snake rivers, Lewis and Clark gave a farewell party for the Nez Percés. Cruzatte played his fiddle while the soldiers square-danced. Sacagawea remembered the first time she had heard Cruzatte's fiddle music and seen the men dance their fancy steps. The Nez Percés, who were as amused as she had once been, then danced for the soldiers.

The company left the Clearwater and started down the Snake River on October 10. The Indians, who fished and boated on the Snake, ran the rapids easily. But Lewis and Clark's men weren't as expert, nor were their canoes as well made. For the next week, they shot over one stretch of boiling rapids after another. Their canoes overturned, ran aground, sprang leaks, were dashed against rocks and capsized. Seams split. Baggage and trade goods got wet or were swept away by the current.

Four days later, the men struggled to keep their canoes afloat over three miles of whitewater rapids. Three of the canoes ran aground, while a fourth got hung up on a boulder. While Twisted Hair swam to shore, the nonswimmers clung to a rock for more than an hour before they could be picked up. Food, gunpowder, bedding and clothes were all lost.

Sacagawea always held Pomp tight in her arms going over the rapids. She had learned to swim as a young girl and she was a strong swimmer. She would make sure that Pomp learned to swim early, too.

After a difficult week of travel on the Snake, the corps sighted the mighty Columbia River. A cheer went up. The Great Father, Thomas Jefferson, had wanted Lewis and Clark to find the Columbia. And they had. Sacagawea was as excited as anyone else. She would soon stand on the shores of the Great Waters.

Their passage down the Columbia River to the Pacific Ocean wouldn't be easy. But no matter how crude and clumsy their dugout canoes were, they had safely brought the Corps of Discovery this far. Now they would just have to make it the rest of the way, no matter what lay ahead.

CHAPTER 16

FACES ALONG THE RIVER

Until the Corps of Discovery had found the Shoshones in August, they hadn't seen a single Indian in more than four months of travel. Then, as they paddled down the Clearwater and Snake rivers, they saw more Indians than they could count. With the rivers teeming with salmon, salmon was king. If the Indians weren't fishing for salmon, they were drying salmon on racks, or pounding dried salmon for trading or winter eating.

Just before the corps turned from the Snake River into the Columbia, two hundred friendly Wanapams arrived for a visit. The Wanapam women were the first real flatheads that Sacagawea, or anyone else, had seen. When they were infants, the girls had their heads flattened between two boards to make a straight line that ran from their noses to the top of their heads.

Sacagawea couldn't imagine flattening her darling Pomp's head. Pomp was eight months old now, sturdy, handsome and strong willed. As soon as she put him down, he crawled away at top speed. With his new baby teeth, his smile charmed everyone, especially Captain Clark.

Because game was scarce, dogmeat stew had lately become the soldiers' food of choice. But Sacagawea refused to eat it. She hadn't eaten horsemeat when she was starving in the mountains, and she wouldn't eat dogmeat now.

The Walla Wallas, who were the first Indians whom the corps met on the Columbia River, were as friendly as the Wanapams had been. Walla Walla Chief Yelleppit, who drew Lewis and Clark a map of the Columbia River on a skin robe, described the hazards that lay ahead. He also described the Indians they would meet. As Twisted Hair and Tetoharsky interpreted, the delighted soldiers traded a few bells, thimbles and beads for forty dogs.

But Indian friendship soon gave way to Indian distrust. On October 19, Clark walked ahead of the canoes, carrying his rifle. While he waited for the others, he shot and killed a crane. The terrified Indians on shore fled into their plank houses. Even with Twisted Hair and Tetoharsky interpreting, Clark couldn't talk them into coming out. It was only when they saw Sacagawea and Pomp arrive in Lewis' canoe that they showed their faces.

Chief Yelleppit had warned Lewis and Clark about

the dangerous fifty-five-mile stretch of the Columbia River that began at Celilo Falls and ended with the rapids of the Cascades. If Sacagawea still wanted adventure, she got it. The fifty-five miles were all roaring waterfalls, narrow channels that wound past towering cliffs, whirlpools, rock-filled shallows and whitewater rapids.

The men had to lower their canoes down Celilo Falls by elk-skin ropes. When they reached the Cascades rapids, the men who couldn't swim walked along the riverbank carrying valuable papers, guns and ammunition. Those men who knew how to swim piloted the canoes.

As the corps battled the raging waters, hundreds of Indians gathered to watch. If only the canoes would smash up on the rocks, they could pick up valuable plunder. What a disappointment that all the canoes made it safely through.

Chief Yelleppit had warned the captains about the Indians. Although different tribes lived along this section of the Columbia River, they were all Chinookan peoples. Their languages were similar and they looked the same, too. The heads of both the men and women were flattened. They were short and squat, with legs swollen from tying cords around their ankles. Some of them wore shells through their noses and some were tattooed, while almost all of them had bad teeth and sore eyes.

The Columbia River was the center of trade for all the northwest tribes. The Chinookans, who were master traders, traded furs with ships on the Pacific coast and had no fear of white men. Because they dominated this section of the Columbia, they considered anything they stole as payment for passage down *their* river. Twisted Hair and Tetoharsky even heard rumors that they planned to kill the whole company.

Sullen and arrogant, the Chinookans agreed to accept trade goods in exchange for dogs, but not for salmon. They saved their many tons of dried salmon to trade for horses, buffalo meat, guns and ammunition, not for trinkets.

The Chinookans did give the company something for free—fleas. Everyone in the corps was crawling with them. Sacagawea stripped off Pomp's clothes to get rid of the fleas, but as soon as she dressed him again, they were back. And Pomp let everyone know in a loud voice just how annoying flea bites were.

Although these people were river pirates, they controlled the food supply. Lewis and Clark had no choice but to get along with them. They even gave a party. Cruzatte played his fiddle and the men square-danced. As always, York was everyone's favorite.

Twisted Hair and Tetoharsky were eager to go home. The Nez Percés and the Chinookan tribes were at war and they would be killed if they stayed. Besides, they didn't know any of the languages farther down the river. After a smoke with Lewis and Clark, the Nez Percé chiefs said their farewells and left.

Like the Nez Percés, Sacagawea heartily distrusted these Chinookans. She avoided them. She watched Pomp's every move.

As a Shoshone, Sacagawea had always been somewhat afraid of the dark. When she was a child, she had been told tales of evil little men known as *NunumBi*. They came out at night and shot arrows of misfortune at anyone who displeased them. A person was safe from the *NunumBi* only while sleeping in a tipi. It helped that she still slept in a tipi with Charbonneau, Pomp, Lewis, Clark and Drouillard. Nevertheless, there was too strong a likeness between the fearful *NunumBi* of her childhood and these little Chinookans. Sacagawea couldn't wait to see the last of them.

CHAPTER 17

POINT DISTRESS

SOON AFTER LEAVING the Columbia River's falls and rapids, the corps sighted a huge rock. Called Beacon Rock, it was a landmark for all sorts of changes. Even though the Pacific Ocean was still more than a hundred miles away, the river now rose and fell with the ocean tides. And when Sacagawea drank the river water, it tasted salty. All oceans are salty, the men told her.

For the first time, they saw seals. Even Sacagawea admitted that they looked almost human. Pomp was fascinated and watched them by the hour. If she hadn't held on to him, he just might have jumped into the river to join them.

The weather changed, too. A dense fog settled down like a blanket. At times, Sacagawea couldn't see fifty steps in front of her. And it never stopped raining. Food spoiled. Bedding and supplies were soaked. Rainwater flooded the canoes. Sacagawea was used to bitter mountain cold and scorching plains heat, but she certainly wasn't used to constant rain. She did her best to keep Pomp dry, but it wasn't possible.

One rainy afternoon, a canoe drew alongside carrying a Chinookan man, his family and a woman prisoner who looked like a Shoshone. Clark sent for Sacagawea to interpret. What an unexpected pleasure. But Sacagawea was disappointed. The woman wasn't a Shoshone after all.

To everyone's surprise, on November 7, 1805, the fog and rain lifted and in the distance they saw what appeared to be the Pacific Ocean. After months of travel and thousands of miles, they had reached their goal. Their journey was over. "O! the joy," Clark wrote in his journal, and joyful was how everyone felt.

Almost right away, they realized their mistake. What they saw wasn't the Pacific. It was still the Columbia River. Because the river up ahead was fifteen miles wide, they hadn't been able to see the riverbanks on either side.

What a painful moment. Although the ocean wasn't far distant, making the final push was hard and the weather didn't help. Gale-force winds blew in rain and hail. The tides ran higher and higher. Swells tumbled and tossed their canoes as waves crashed over them. Huge driftwood logs pitched and rolled in the water.

Almost the whole party was seasick. Sacagawea threw up over the side like everyone else. If only she could get out on land maybe her stomach would settle down.

Lewis and Clark finally called a halt on November 10. If the waves didn't swamp their canoes, then the driftwood would crush them. For the next five days, the company camped on the north side of the river. They hunted in the rain, ate in the rain and slept in the rain. Fires were hard to start and even harder to keep going. Sacagawea agreed with the others that it was the most miserable campsite yet. Clark gave it a perfect name, Point Distress.

Unlike the soldiers, the Indians could handle the worst that the river or the weather threw at them. Some of their handsomely carved oceangoing canoes were fifty feet long and could hold as many as thirty people. Known as Chinooks, these Indians were related to the Chinookan tribes the corps had met earlier.

Many of the Chinooks wore white-men's clothing. Some of them had even picked up a few words of English from sailors on American ships. But just like their Chinookan cousins, these coastal Chinooks were sullen, disagreeable and tough traders. With no game to be found, Lewis and Clark had to trade top-value goods for dried salmon and wapato roots. Sacagawea was especially fond of wapato roots, which were like small potatoes and delicious when roasted.

On November 15, after eleven straight days of rain, the weather cleared and the corps pushed off along the riverbank. They went only another four miles to a campsite that was on higher and hopefully drier ground. Nearby were a number of empty flea-filled Indian houses which provided wood for a shelter. In turn, the corps, especially Seaman, provided housing for the fleas.

From their new campsite, the Corps of Discovery could at last see the Pacific Ocean, a far-off slate gray sea under a slate gray sky. Breakers and waves crashed against the shoreline. Sacagawea, and everyone else, was past celebrating. They were waterlogged and dead tired from fighting the waves and bailing out their canoes. All their belongings were wet. Their rotted clothes hung in tatters. Weary, wet and numb, they considered it was victory enough that they had made it.

CHAPTER 18

GENEROSITY

FOR THE NEXT TEN DAYS, the pounding waves and fierce winds trapped the corps in their camp on the north shore of the Columbia River. Although there was no game to be found, nearby friendly Clatsop Indians sold them wapato roots and dried fish.

The Chinooks made their usual trouble. Although Sacagawea wanted nothing to do with them, that wasn't always possible. A Chinook chief showed up one day wearing a magnificent robe made of sea otter skins. Both Lewis and Clark wanted the robe, and wanted it badly. But the chief would trade his robe only for blue beads and the company's blue beads were almost gone. Unfortunately, the chief noticed Sacagawea's lovely blue-beaded belt and gestured to it.

Everyone, including Sacagawea, knew what the chief wanted. He would trade his robe for her belt. All Indians prized blue beads, which they called "chief beads," and Sacagawea treasured her belt. She shuddered to think of this little Chinook *NunumBi* wearing it.

Nevertheless, she couldn't refuse. She owed Lewis and Clark everything. They had given her wings to fly on this adventure. More than that, Lewis had helped her through Pomp's difficult birth and had saved her life when she was desperately sick. Back at the Great Falls, Clark had rescued Pomp and her from drowning. She untied her belt and gave it to the Chinook chief. Considering all that the captains had done for her, Sacagawea didn't consider her generosity to be anything special.

Although Lewis and Clark gave Sacagawea a blue cloth coat in exchange for her belt, they didn't make much of her generosity either. They were concerned about a more serious matter. It was already the end of November and they still hadn't found a site for their winter headquarters. The two captains went off in different directions to explore the coastline.

After five days, they returned. They offered the company three choices. The Corps of Discovery could spend the winter on the north shore, where they were now. They could return to Celilo Falls and camp there. Or they could move to the south side of the river, where the friendly Clatsops lived and timber and game were more plentiful.

Shoshone women had always had a voice in village

decisions. Sacagawea intended to have a voice in this decision, too. And she did. Janey, as Clark always called her, voted to cross the river to the south side. Being practical, she added that she wanted to camp where there was plenty of wapato. Charbonneau was the only one who didn't vote. Like Sacagawea, most of the men elected to move to the south shore.

The next day the corps made it across the Columbia River to the south shore. But they had to camp on the riverbank for more than a week while Lewis and five men searched for a site for their winter fort. As they waited, rains and winds battered them. Most of the men fell sick, including Clark. Sacagawea had been saving a piece of bread made from flour as a treat for Pomp. Thoughtful as ever, she gave it to Clark instead. It was the first bread that he had tasted in months and he ate it with pleasure.

Two days later, one of the hunters returned with an elk he had shot. Even though the elk meat would have given him strength, Clark was too sick to eat it. Sacagawea knew just what to do. After chopping up two large elk bones, she boiled them and skimmed the fat off the top. The men had lived for weeks on dried fish and roots. Cold, wet and sickly, they all craved animal fat to give them energy. Just the smell of the sizzling elk fat picked up everyone's spirits, especially Clark's.

Lewis and his men returned on December 7 with

good news. They had found just the right site. It was three miles south of the Columbia River on high, dry ground, with a spring nearby. A dense growth of spruce trees would supply both firewood and lumber for their headquarters. They had seen plenty of elk and game in the area.

The corps had spent almost a month moving from one soggy river camp to another. Sacagawea had endured those miserable weeks with grace and generosity. Now she packed Pomp's damp bedding and clothes. Still uncomplaining, she buttoned up her blue coat, ready for whatever the coming winter had in store for them.

CHAPTER 19

LONG, WET AND BORING

THE WINTER OF 1805–6 turned out to be long, wet and boring. Endless days of rain and fog kept everyone inside. Their diet of roasted elk, dried elk, boiled elk and leftover elk quickly grew tiresome. The Clatsops, who brought fish, wapato roots and sometimes a dog or two to trade, didn't even know sign language. Fort Clatsop began to seem like a prison.

The men had built Fort Clatsop with two rows of cabins, four on one side and three on the other, with a parade ground in the middle and a stockade fence all around. Actually, Sacagawea was delighted with the arrangement. For the first time since leaving Fort Mandan, she and her little family had their own living quarters.

But Sacagawea was used to cold, snowy winters, not months of rain, fog and mist. The cabins were always damp. Clothes and bedding mildewed. Everyone came down with colds, coughs and flu. Fleas were a torment. Game spoiled even before the hunters could bring it back to the fort.

Some of the men worked at a salt-making camp fifteen miles down the coast. They boiled seawater in huge kettles until the kettles were coated with salt. They then scraped off the salt and stored it in kegs. They used the salt to flavor their food and preserve game from the hunt.

Sacagawea, and the men who weren't making salt, spent the winter mending their clothes and sewing new breeches, shirts and moccasins. To kill time, they turned out more moccasins than they could possibly use, 338 pairs.

Although Sacagawea had seen the captains write in their journals during the trip, Lewis now wrote for hours every day. He told her that he was describing everything they had seen: animals, birds, fish, insects and plants, as well as all the Indian tribes they had met. Clark passed the winter drawing maps. And the two men talked endlessly about what route they would take on their return trip.

Pomp was by far the happiest member of the company. During the winter, he learned first to stand up, and then to walk. He was terribly pleased with himself and laughed even when he fell. Sacagawea had lots of help taking care of him. The men played with him by the hour and even taught him to dance.

At least Christmas Day, 1805, was a break. The Christmas before, Sacagawea had been puzzled by the singing, shouting, shooting and exchanging of gifts. This year she was prepared.

When the corps had stayed with the Shoshones, the men had admired the warriors' handsome white ermine capes. During her time with Cameahwait, Sacagawea had gotten hold of two dozen white ermine tails. Now she gave them to her special friend, Captain Clark. She knew that he would be pleased and he was. The ermine tails were even more beautiful than the sea otter robe that the Chinook chief had traded for her blue-beaded belt. Aside from the exchanging of gifts, Christmas wasn't much. Dinner was spoiled elk, roots and rotten fish, with nothing to drink but water.

Although Sacagawea didn't expect thanks for her gift, she did expect to be treated fairly. But she wasn't. Only two weeks after Christmas, the salt-making crew returned with news that a whale had been washed ashore farther down the coast. Whale blubber could be boiled to make oil and when it was cooked, it was quite tasty.

Clark and eleven men made plans to travel down the coast, take a look at the whale and bring back blubber and oil. When Sacagawea heard that she wasn't included, she turned on Clark. He hadn't even asked if she wanted to go. She was as bored and tired of the rain as anyone else. She had never seen the Great Waters except at a distance. Now there was a monstrous fish to be seen as well. Captain Clark had no right to leave her behind.

The soldiers were astounded. They had never heard Sacagawea scold anyone, let alone Captain Clark.

In response to Clark's hasty invitation, Sacagawea, Charbonneau and Pomp were ready early the next morning. The party covered the thirty-five miles down to the whale in two days, first by canoe and then on foot. On the second day, they followed a Clatsop guide up a steep, twelve-hundred-foot-high bluff that jutted out into the ocean.

The view from the top was more spectacular than anything that Sacagawea had ever seen. A raging sea spread out before her, all wind-whipped waves and booming surf. Breakers crashed in a line of white foam along the shoreline. Seals basked on the rocks or bobbed in the mountainous swells.

When Clark's party reached the whale, the men were disappointed to find that the Indians had stripped it clean. Sacagawea was perfectly content just to see what was left. She could hardly believe that any creature could be so huge. Clark, of course, measured the remains. The skeleton was a hundred and five feet long, he reported. With the trade goods he had brought with him, he bargained with the Indians for three hundred pounds of blubber and some oil.

The four-day whale trip was the beginning, and end, of Sacagawea and anyone else's adventures. The dreary days dragged on. Lewis and Clark had planned to leave on April 1, but by the middle of March they couldn't take any more. Of their four months on the coast, only twelve days had been without rain.

They were in such a hurry to leave, in fact, that they stole an Indian canoe. Stealing from the Indians had always been forbidden. The theft surprised Sacagawea, but the men didn't care. They were just happy to be done with the rain, boredom and elk meat of Fort Clatsop. They had, after all, signed up for the Journey of Discovery as soldiers, not salt-makers or tailors.

On March 23, 1806, the two captains turned the fort over to their favorite Clatsop chief. The men loaded the five canoes and they pushed off for their return passage.

Sacagawea agreed that the winter had been long, wet and boring but it hadn't been a waste of time. She had stood on the shores of the Great Waters. She had seen the remains of a monstrous fish. They were sights that she would never forget.

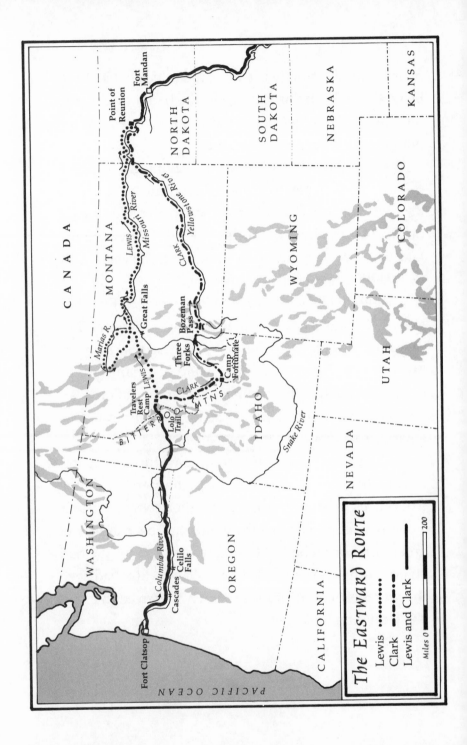

The Eastward Route

Lewis ·············
Clark ▪▪▪▪▪▪▪
Lewis and Clark ━━━━

Miles 0 ━━━━ 200

CHAPTER 20

UPSTREAM TERROR

ALTHOUGH LEWIS AND CLARK WERE IN A HURRY, travel on the Columbia River was slow. Instead of going with the current, they were now going against it. Melted snow coming down from the mountains had raised the river ten feet and the rain never let up.

At least for a few weeks the local Indians were friendly. By chance, on their first day out, they asked directions from an Indian who recognized the canoe they had stolen. It was his. Luckily, he was willing to accept an elk skin in payment.

Sacagawea knew that the Indians wouldn't be friendly for long. And they weren't. As the corps covered the miles, more and more curious Chinookans gathered along the riverbanks. They paddled their canoes up close. At night they hung around the company's campfires, much like the Shoshone *NunumBi*.

Other Indian tribes had been pleased to see Sacagawea and Pomp traveling with the white men. The

Chinookans didn't give her a second glance. Just the sight of five canoes filled with white strangers enraged them. They were even more hostile than they had been the fall before. Their winter supply of dried fish was gone and the salmon hadn't yet returned to the Columbia River. They were starving, which made Sacagawea uneasy. She knew how hunger could turn people inside out and backward, and even well-fed Chinookans were nasty.

To pass through the four miles of terrible chutes and rapids of the Cascades, the soldiers had to walk on shore and tow their canoes. Indians pelted them from above with rocks. They pushed one of the soldiers off the path and grabbed the dog he had bought for his dinner. Knives and tomahawks were stolen. The men were insulted and pestered. Tempers on both sides began to boil over.

And then three Indians made off with Lewis' dog. Lewis was furious. He ordered three men to get Seaman back even if they had to shoot the thieves. Fortunately, when the Indians saw the armed soldiers following them, they let Seaman go. Lewis then told his men that if the Indians tried to steal anything else, or even if they insulted a member of the corps, they had his permission to shoot.

With that order, Sacagawea knew they were in trouble. Lewis had lost his temper. Sacagawea understood hotheaded men. She was, after all, married to Charbonneau. Long ago, she had learned to keep quiet when he flew into a rage.

Although Sacagawea stayed quiet now, she could have told Lewis that they were only thirty-three people surrounded by hundreds of starving, angry warriors. The Chinookans could wipe out their whole party and no one would ever know what had happened to them. Lewis should smile and be friendly. He should tell Cruzatte to play his fiddle so that the men could dance. Even better, Lewis should let the Chinookans steal a few knives and axes.

But Lewis had no such plans. When he caught another Chinookan stealing, he beat him and had him thrown out of camp. He then made it clear to the watching Indians that he wasn't afraid to fight them. He could kill them all.

The Chinookans ignored the threat and continued to steal. They were rulers of this river and no white man was going to tell them what to do. Even after Lewis warned that he would burn down their village if they didn't return an army blanket, they paid no attention.

When the blanket was found in one of the lodges, Sacagawea breathed easier. If Lewis had set the village on fire, Indians all up and down the river would have attacked in a rage. She guarded Pomp more closely than ever and didn't let him out of her sight. When he toddled off, even for a moment, she flew after him.

The soldiers' tempers rose along with Lewis'. Killing was on their minds, too. Sacagawea didn't like the way they slept with their guns in their arms. A sudden noise might startle them into firing at anyone or anything.

The stealing got worse. Conditions on the river also got worse. Lewis and Clark didn't have the manpower to fight the current and the rapids and still post guards. They had no choice but to continue their journey on foot. Although the company picked up ten packhorses from the surly Chinookans over the next eight days, they had to trade their best goods, including two valuable cooking kettles. Sacagawea gave Charbonneau two of her elk-skin garments to trade for a horse. She would have given up anything to be on her way.

Finally, on April 24, 1806, the Corps of Discovery got rid of the last of their canoes and started out for Nez Percé country on foot. Sacagawea had been edgy for weeks. Now the danger was past. Pomp was safe. They had seen the last of the *NunumBi* . . . forever.

CHAPTER 21

TRUE HAPPINESS

EVERYONE'S FEET WERE SORE from walking over rough stones and deep sand. Because each step took her farther away from the Chinookans, Sacagawea didn't mind. Three days later, on April 27, 1806, their old friend Chief Yelleppit and his Walla Wallas welcomed the corps. Sacagawea returned their warm greeting. This was more like it.

The Walla Wallas were holding a Shoshone woman prisoner. When Sacagawea spoke to the woman in her native language, it was like coming home. Even better, Sacagawea could be useful again. Lewis and Clark wanted her to interpret through the Shoshone woman, who also understood Walla Walla. The talk went from Walla Walla to Shoshone, from Shoshone to Minnetaree, from Minnetaree to French and from French to English. It was slow, but Lewis and Clark could express themselves better than they could in sign language.

Before the corps left his camp, Yelleppit threw a

celebration. Cruzatte brought out his battered old fiddle and the soldiers all danced. Then the Indians danced. Even little Pomp danced. No wonder Clark called him "my little dancing boy."

Four days after leaving the Walla Wallas with twenty-three fresh horses, the corps arrived in Nez Percé country. The first Nez Percé they met was Tetoharsky, who had been their guide last fall.

All the Nez Percés were happy to see the company again. Word had spread that the previous year Clark had cured an old man who had been unable to walk. Now Nez Percés lined up to be doctored by the Red-headed Chief in every village they passed through. He treated broken bones, sprains, boils, ulcers and sore eyes. In payment, the Nez Percés gave him horses, dogs, roots and berries.

Like the Walla Wallas, the Nez Percés were holding a Shoshone prisoner, this time a young boy. Once again Sacagawea interpreted. Lewis and Clark gave the same speech that they had given to every tribe along their route. They told the Nez Percés that they came from a large and powerful nation. Their Great Father wanted all the Indians to live in peace. And the Nez Percés could look forward to American trading posts that would bring them needed goods coming soon.

In turn, the Nez Percés had advice for the captains.

They shouldn't try to cross the mountains on the Lolo Trail for at least a month. Sacagawea could have told them that herself. She had spent enough winters in the Rocky Mountains to know that even in May, deep snow still blocked the mountain passes.

On May 14, the corps set up camp on the Clearwater River to wait for the snow to melt. They also had to wait for their old friend and guide Twisted Hair to round up the horses they had left in his care last October.

Sacagawea remembered how sick the men had been the year before from eating camas roots and dried fish. She set right to work digging up tender spring fennel and yampa roots. Some of the roots she cooked, and some she dried. She gathered wild onions, too, which she boiled to eat with meat.

Sacagawea was having a good time. She chatted in Shoshone with the young prisoner and she enjoyed digging roots with the other women. Pomp had been cranky for a few days but she didn't think much about it. He was teething and that always made him fussy. Then he was more than fussy. He was sick. He woke up on May 22 with a high fever. His neck and jaw were swollen. He could hardly swallow.

Sacagawea never left his side. She tried to nurse him but he wasn't hungry. She rocked and sang to him but he was in too much pain to sleep. Just last year,

Sacagawea had been near death herself. Now she would give her life to have her son well again.

Charbonneau was worried, too, but there was nothing he could do. Lewis and Clark couldn't do much either. This wasn't a simple cold or stomachache. They kept hot poultices of wild onions on Pomp's neck and jaw. They tried one medicine after another to bring down the swelling.

After a few days, Pomp's fever was gone and he seemed better. But the next morning he was sicker than ever. Although the two captains were afraid that he might die, Sacagawea refused to consider such a possibility.

The two captains doubled their efforts. Clark, who always called Pomp "my boy Pomp," was especially concerned. Finally, Pomp began to improve. Each day he was a little stronger. At last he was out of danger and the swelling was gone.

Sacagawea had thought that she was happy to come on this adventure . . . to be reunited with her Shoshone band . . . to see the Great Waters . . . to pass safely through Chinookan country. Now she realized that she had never known what real happiness was. Real happiness was when her little boy ran into her arms laughing. Never again would she take her happiness for granted.

CHAPTER 22

LESSONS TO BE LEARNED

SACAGAWEA AND EVERYONE ELSE could see the snow-covered Bitterroot range of the Rocky Mountains from their camp. The Nez Percés again warned Lewis and Clark that the snow was too deep to make it over the Lolo Trail. Sacagawea agreed. But Lewis and Clark wouldn't listen. They couldn't wait to get started. When the Nez Percés realized that the two captains planned to leave anyway, they offered to send some men to guide them.

Lewis and Clark didn't want to wait for the Nez Percé guides either. They would go on their own. Drouillard was a fine woodsman. He would lead them. Besides, they had been over the Lolo Trail last fall with Old Toby and they knew the way.

Sacagawea was astonished. Of course Lewis and Clark didn't know the way. They should listen to the Nez Percés . . . or to her. Anyone who had lived in these parts would tell them that it was still too early in the season to cross the mountains.

But Lewis and Clark were determined. They led the corps toward the Bitterroots on June 15, 1806, with sixty-six good horses, thanks to the Nez Percés' generosity. Each person was mounted and leading a packhorse. Fearing what lay ahead, Sacagawea had made sure that her little family had plenty of warm clothing, especially Pomp. He seemed to feel like his old self, but she didn't want to take any chances.

They made good time the first day. The second day was slower. The Lolo Trail was covered with eight to ten feet of crusty snow. Although the horses sank in only two or three inches, grass was hard to find. The next day was worse. The snow was twelve to fifteen feet deep and there was no grass at all. And it was bitterly cold. Sacagawea constantly checked Pomp's cheeks to make sure they weren't frostbitten.

Without grass, the horses couldn't survive, and without horses, the corps couldn't survive. Lewis and Clark had no choice. They had to turn back. It was their first retreat. As they headed down the mountain, the men's mood was black. Not Sacagawea's. Retreating was the best decision the two captains had made in weeks.

Nine days after their first try, they started out again. This time, Nez Percé guides were with them, as well as three more Nez Percés who had joined their party. Although the snow had melted a couple of feet, it was still deep. Luckily, it was solid enough to hold the horses' weight. Because the ground was bare in places, Sacagawea dug for roots. She found the tasty white roots that the men had earlier said were like Jerusalem artichokes.

Sacagawea was sure that the Nez Percé guides would be skilled woodsmen and they were. They planned each day's travel according to where grass could be found for the horses. One day there was no grass. The Nez Percés promised the worried captains that by noon the following day they would reach grass. And they did.

By June 29, they were out of the snow at the Lolo Trail's warm springs. What a treat! The Indians had blocked up the river to make a warm pool. To sink into the bubbling hot water was to feel renewed. Sacagawea took off all of Pomp's clothes and let him splash and kick to his heart's content.

Late the next afternoon, the party reached Travelers Rest, where they had camped nine months before. The Bitterroot range was behind them. The Nez Percé guides had led them more than 150 miles in only six days through deep snow and dense forest without ever losing the trail. Sacagawea was in awe of their perfect sense of direction, timing and distance. The year before, the corps had barely survived eleven days of blizzards, accidents and near starvation.

On the other hand, Sacagawea was troubled by the two captains. Clark was her good friend and she respected Lewis. Yet both men obviously considered themselves to be superior to Indians. They talked to Indians as if they were children, treated them like children and even called them "dutiful children." They had certainly had plenty of proof by now that Indians were better horsemen, rivermen and woodsmen than any soldier in their corps.

Back at Fort Mandan, the Mandans and Minnetarees had helped the expedition get off to a good start. Her own Shoshone people had shared what little they had. The Nez Percés had taken them in, fed them, traded their best horses and sent expert guides to lead them. It was about time that the captains realized how much the Indians had to teach them. But they would first have to open their minds, and their hearts, too, if they wanted to learn.

CHAPTER 23

DANGEROUS DECISIONS

THE CORPS SPENT THREE DAYS AT TRAVELERS REST. There, Lewis and Clark announced their plans. Lewis and one group would follow the Missouri River to the Great Falls, then continue north to explore the Marias River. Clark and another group would head south and pick up the canoes they had sunk at Camp Fortunate. From there, they would explore and map the Yellowstone River.

Sacagawea couldn't imagine what the captains were thinking of. Both parties would be going deep into enemy Indian territory. Splitting up would put everyone at risk. Lewis and Clark had been ordered to find a route to the Great Waters and they had done it. Now it was time to go home.

Nevertheless, on July 3, 1806, the two captains started out in different directions. Lewis, nine men, his dog, Seaman, and seventeen horses headed east toward the

Missouri River. Clark, Sacagawea, Pomp, Charbonneau, York and eighteen men with forty-nine horses rode south.

At least for the time being, Sacagawea was riding through familiar Shoshone countryside. Although she hoped against hope that she would see her people again, in her heart she knew she wouldn't. At this time of year, they were camped in the mountains. Sadly, she knew she had seen her family and friends for the last time.

When the Shoshone tracks they were following across a wide plain became scattered, Sacagawea led the way. She told Clark they would find a gap in the mountains ahead that would lead them to Camp Fortunate.

Just as Sacagawea had predicted, on July 8, Clark's party arrived at Camp Fortunate. The summer before, they had sunk their canoes in the Beaverhead River and cached food, supplies and tobacco. Sacagawea had to laugh. The men couldn't get to the tobacco fast enough. They had run out of tobacco four months ago and they were desperate.

While the men worked on the canoes, Sacagawea dug up some of the Shoshones' favorite roots, which looked and tasted like carrots. Two days later, they followed the Beaverhead River into the Jefferson. Although half the party rode and half canoed, they kept each other in sight. When they reached the familiar Beaver's Head rock, Sacagawea again knew just where they were. So far, so good. There had been no sign of enemy Indians.

But when they reached the Missouri River at Three Forks on July 13, Clark once again split up their party. Clark, Sacagawea, Pomp, Charbonneau, York and eight men would ride to the Yellowstone River with all the horses. The other ten men would take the canoes down the Missouri to meet Lewis' men at the Great Falls. The two groups parted.

Sacagawea was well aware that as their party got smaller, the danger grew greater. Hurry, they had to hurry. At least they had good horses and the countryside was still familiar. They forded the Madison River and rode across an open plain crisscrossed by buffalo trails that led to a gap in the mountains some twenty miles away. Sacagawea pointed to another gap in the mountains farther south. She told Clark that traveling through that pass would get them to the Yellowstone River in better time.

Sacagawea hadn't let Clark down yet and she didn't let him down this time. With Sacagawea as their guide, they forded the many branches of the Gallatin River and followed a buffalo trail across an open plain. The next day they rode over the mountain pass, later named

Bozeman Pass, and arrived at the Yellowstone River. Sacagawea had successfully led the party for more than forty miles.

But they were in the heart of Crow country. Crows were the Shoshones' bitter enemies and Sacagawea was fearful, more for Pomp than for herself. During the next two days they saw a Crow watching them and Crow smoke signals in the distance.

Crow country or not, after four days of following the Yellowstone on horseback, Clark had his little party stop to make two canoes. The Crows were master horse thieves, as Sacagawea well knew. That night, they crept into camp and stole twenty-four of the company's best horses.

When the two canoes were finally finished, Clark split the party again. Four soldiers were to take what horses hadn't been stolen and ride back to Fort Mandan with a message. Sacagawea was astonished. They were surrounded by Crows, and Clark was allowing their party to dwindle down to seven men, Pomp and herself.

At least they made good time traveling with the current. They even enjoyed a pleasant stopover. They saw a huge rock formation by the Yellowstone riverbank. Clark climbed its two-hundred-foot height and carved his name and date in the rock, "W^M Clark July 25 1806."

He also named the rock Pompy's Tower after little Pomp, whom he adored.

Pomp was a year and a half old now and no longer a baby. He had never known any life but being on the move and he was happy to ride, sit in a canoe or simply be carried. But he wasn't happy when they ran into their old foe, mosquitoes. They had never been worse and sleep was impossible. Poor Pomp's face was bloated and swollen from bites.

Although Lewis and Clark had planned to meet where the Yellowstone and Missouri rivers joined, the mosquitoes were unbearable. Clark left a note on a stick for Lewis and headed his little party in their two canoes down the Missouri.

Five days later, to everyone's surprise, the four soldiers whom Clark had sent back to Fort Mandan weeks before came floating down the river behind them. The Crows had stolen all their horses. The men had promptly made circular buffalo-skin boats just like Indian bull boats and pushed off into the Missouri River to find Clark. Sacagawea was impressed. Someone had finally learned a thing or two from the Indians.

At last, on August 12, 1806, Lewis, his nine men plus the ten men, who had met them earlier at the Great Falls, came in sight. They were riding in five canoes and the white pirogue which they had picked up at the

Great Falls. Forty days had passed since the corps had separated. Sacagawea had doubted that they would ever see one another again. Yet here all thirty-three of them were back together. She was thankful that everyone had survived. And she was thankful that they didn't have far to go. There wouldn't be time for the captains to make any more foolish decisions.

CHAPTER 24

A SAD FAREWELL

LEWIS AND HIS PARTY had had quite a story to tell. After reaching the Great Falls, Lewis and three men had traveled by horseback up the Marias River deep into enemy Blackfoot territory.

The Blackfeet had stolen seven of their horses and then tried to steal their guns. All of a sudden, Lewis and his three men had found themselves in a running battle. The captains' standing orders were never to shoot or harm an Indian. But one of the soldiers had fatally stabbed a warrior, while Lewis had seriously wounded another. To escape, Lewis and his men had ridden more than a hundred miles straight, stopping only to rest their horses.

Lewis' troubles weren't over. Picking up the rest of his party at the Great Falls, as well as the white pirogue, Lewis had led his nineteen men to the mouth of the Marias River. But when they had uncovered the red pirogue which they had hidden the year before, it wasn't usable. There was nothing to do but head down the Missouri River in the five canoes and the white pirogue to meet Clark.

On their way, Lewis and Cruzatte had stopped to hunt elk. As usual, Lewis was wearing his buckskin shirt and breeches. When Cruzatte, who had poor eyesight, saw what he thought was an elk, he fired. His bullet ripped into Lewis' right buttock and came out the left, leaving a painful wound.

When Sacagawea heard Lewis' story, she considered him fortunate. First, he had made it out of Blackfoot country with his life. Second, Cruzatte's bullet had only wounded him.

Two days after Lewis and Clark were reunited, the first Minnetaree village came in sight. Minnetarees lined both sides of the Missouri River to watch the little fleet arrive.

When the Minnetarees told Lewis and Clark that Fort Mandan had burned down in a prairie fire, the corps set up camp on the riverbank. With Lewis still unable to walk, Clark made all the arrangements for their leave-taking. A Mandan chief and his family were traveling with them to meet the Great Father in Washington, with René Jesseaume and his family going along to interpret.

Calling Pomp a "beautiful, promising child," Clark asked Sacagawea and Charbonneau if he could take little Pomp back to live with him in St. Louis. The answer was no. Pomp was too young. But maybe he could come next year.

On the day that the corps left, Clark paid Charbonneau his wages, $500.33, which included the price of a horse and a lodge. During their sixteen-month journey, Charbonneau had contributed next to nothing. He had not only been the worst riverman in the company, but he was also a poor horseman. He had been thrown from his mount more than once and he had delayed the party two times by losing his horse. In pursuit of a buffalo, he and his horse had fallen and he had been badly bruised. Going over the Bitterroots, a packhorse loaded with trade goods had gotten away from Charbonneau and fallen in a mountain stream. All the trade goods had either been soaked or carried away by the current.

Although Sacagawea received no pay at all, she had contributed far more than had been asked of her. She had been steady in a crisis, generous, uncomplaining, helpful as a guide and essential in dealing with the Shoshones. She had also brought a sense of home and family to the corps. Over and over, her presence had let the Indians know that the expedition was peaceable. By digging roots and gathering berries and fruit, she had improved the men's diet and picked up their spirits. Through it all, she had raised a happy, healthy child.

Clark was well aware of all that Sacagawea had done. He later wrote to Charbonneau that Janey, as he still called her, "deserved a greater reward for her attention and services on that route than we had in our power to give her."

After only a three-day stopover, on August 17, 1806, Lewis, Clark and their Corps of Discovery started down the Missouri River for home. Sacagawea, Charbonneau, Pomp and hundreds of Mandans and Minnetarees came to see them off. As Sacagawea watched the canoes and the white pirogue sweep downstream, she realized that her Journey of Discovery was really, truly over. But what an adventure it had been.

Along with the men, she had suffered through freezing cold, scorching heat, teeming rain, near starvation, illness, accidents, boredom, moments of terror, grizzly bears and mosquitoes.

More to the point, she had also experienced new friendships, joy, laughter, unforgettable sights and good times. She had seen family and friends she had once thought she would never see again. She had stood on the shores of the Great Waters, learned how other tribes lived and had the satisfaction of knowing she had been useful. In other words, she had been given wings. Her life would never be the same again.

EPILOGUE

ALTHOUGH LITTLE IS KNOWN about the rest of Sacagawea's life, it is known that she, Pomp and Charbonneau traveled to St. Louis sometime between 1807 and 1810. Charbonneau bought property from William Clark in October, 1810, but apparently living in St. Louis didn't appeal to him. Five months later he sold the property back.

Leaving Pomp in Clark's care, Charbonneau and Sacagawea returned to their Minnetaree village in April, 1811. A passenger on their boat going up the Missouri River commented that Sacagawea was "a good creature, of a mild and gentle disposition, greatly attached to the whites." He also commented that she was "sickly and longed to revisit her native country."

In August, 1812, Sacagawea gave birth to a daughter, Lizette. Charbonneau was then working as a trapper and fur trader at Fort Manuel on the Missouri River. Sacagawea died at the fort on December 20, 1812, and was buried there. The Fort Manuel clerk wrote: "This evening the wife of Charbonneau, a Snake [Shoshone] squaw, died of a putrid fever. She was a good and the best woman in the fort, aged about 25 years. She left a fine infant girl."

Another version of her life story contends that Sacagawea died in 1884 on Wind River Shoshone Reservation in Wyoming. She would have been almost one hundred years old. Historians, however, have basically disproved this account.

William Clark took Pomp into his home, became his legal guardian and educated him. Baptiste, as Pomp became known, attracted the attention of a German prince who was traveling in America. In 1824, the prince took nineteen-year-old Baptiste back to Europe with him for six years. But the frontier beckoned, and Baptiste returned to the west. He spent the rest of his life as a fur trader, guide and mountain man. He died in 1866.

Charbonneau worked as an interpreter, trapper, fur trader and guide all over the west until his death in his eighties. He lost all contact with both Baptiste and Lizette.

BIBLIOGRAPHY

AMBROSE, STEPHEN E. *Undaunted Courage.* New York: Simon & Schuster, 1996.

APPLEMAN, ROY E. *Lewis and Clark.* Washington, D.C.: United States Department of the Interior, National Park Service, 1975.

BAKELESS, JOHN, ED. *The Journals of Lewis and Clark.* New York: Mentor, 1964.

BOSS, RICHARD C. "Keelboat, Pirogue, and Canoe: Vessels Used by the Lewis and Clark Corps of Discovery." *Nautical Research Journal,* June 1993.

BRACKENRIDGE, HENRY M. *Journal of a Voyage up the Missouri River in 1811.* Baltimore: Coale and Maxwell, 1816.

BURT, OLIVE. *Sacagawea.* New York: Franklin Watts, 1978.

CATLIN, GEORGE. *The Manners, Customs, and Conditions of the North American Indians.* Vols. I, II. London: Published by the Author, 1841.

Chuinard, E. G. *Only One Man Died: The Medical Aspects of the Lewis and Clark Expedition.* Glendale, CA: The Arthur H. Clark Company, 1979.

Clark, Ella E., and Margot Edmonds. *Sacagawea of the Lewis and Clark Expedition.* Berkeley, CA: University of California Press, 1979.

Coues, Elliott, ed. *The History of the Lewis and Clark Expedition.* Vols. I, II, III. New York: Dover Publications, Inc., 1987.

DeVoto, Bernard. *The Course of Empire.* Boston: Houghton Mifflin Company, 1952.

————, ed. *The Journals of Lewis and Clark.* Boston: Houghton Mifflin Company, 1953.

Eide, Ingvard Henry. *American Odyssey: The Journey of Lewis and Clark.* Chicago: Rand McNally & Company, 1969.

Gass, Patrick. *A Journal of the Voyages and Travels of a Corps of Discovery under the Command of Captain Lewis and Captain Clark.* Edited by David McKeehan. Minneapolis: Ross and Haines Co., 1958.

Gilman, Carolyn, and Mary Jane Schneider. *The Way to Independence: Memories of a Hidatsa Indian Family, 1840–1920.* St. Paul, MN: Minnesota Historical Society Press, 1987.

Haines, Francis. *The Nez Percés.* Norman, OK: University of Oklahoma Press, 1955.

Hawke, David Freeman. *Those Tremendous Mountains: The Story of the Lewis and Clark Expedition.* New York: W. W. Norton & Company, 1980.

Hebard, Grace Raymond. *Sacajawea.* Glendale, CA: The Arthur H. Clark Company, 1933.

Holloway, David. *Lewis & Clark and the Crossing of North America.* New York: Saturday Review Press, 1974.

Howard, Harold P. *Sacajawea.* Norman, OK: University of Oklahoma Press, 1971.

Jackson, Donald, ed. *Letters of the Lewis and Clark Expedition with Related Documents 1783–1854.* Urbana, IL: University of Illinois Press, 1962.

Josephy, Alvin M., Jr. *The Nez Percé Indians and the Opening of the Northwest.* New Haven: Yale University Press, 1965.

Lavender, David. *The Way to the Western Sea: Lewis and Clark Across the Continent.* New York: Harper & Row, Publishers, 1988.

Luttig, John C. *Journal of a Fur-Trading Expedition on the Upper Missouri 1812–1813.* Edited by Stella M. Drummer. New York: Argosy-Antiquarian Ltd., 1964.

Meyer, Roy W. *The Village Indians of the Upper Missouri.* Lincoln: University of Nebraska Press, 1977.

Moulton, Gary E., ed. *The Journals of the Lewis & Clark*

Expedition. Vols. 3, 4, 5, 6, 7, 8. Lincoln, NB: University of Nebraska Press, 1986–1993.

MURPHY, DAN. *Lewis and Clark: Voyage of Discovery.* Las Vegas, NV: KC Publications, 1977.

QUAIFE, MILO, ED. *Journals of Cap't. Meriwether Lewis and Sergeant John Ordway.* Vol. XXII. Madison, WI: Wisconsin Historical Publications, 1916.

REID, RUSSELL. *Sakakawea: The Bird Woman.* Bismarck, ND: State Historical Society of North Dakota, 1986.

RONDA, JAMES P. *Lewis and Clark Among the Indians.* Lincoln, NB: University of Nebraska Press, 1974.

———. "A Most Perfect Harmony: Life at Fort Mandan." *We Proceeded On,* vol. 14, no. 4 (November 1988).

THWAITES, REUBEN GOLD, ED. *Original Journals of the Lewis and Clark Expedition.* Vols. 2, 3, 4, 5. New York: Arno Press, 1969.

TRENHOLM, VIRGINIA COLE, AND MAURINE CARLEY. *The Shoshonis: Sentinels of the Rockies.* Norman, OK: University of Oklahoma Press, 1964.

INDEX

Beaverhead River, 44, 51, 52
Birds, 28
Bird Woman, 4. *See also* Sacagawea
Bitterroot mountains, 56, 93–96
Blackfeet Indians, 103
Blue beads, 75–76
Boating accident, 25–26

Camas roots, 59–60, 91
Cameahwait, 49–50, 51–54
Camp Fortunate, 51–53, 98
Canoes, 42, 52, 60–63, 98, 100, 104
  stolen from Indians, 83, 85
Charbonneau, Jean Baptiste
    (Pomp), 16, 17, 20, 48,
    51–52, 53, 66–67, 69, 71, 101
  boating accident, 25–26
  Clark and, 105, 107–8
  dancing, 90
  first winter, 80–81
  flash flood incident, 38–40
  illness of, 91–92
Charbonneau, Lizette, 107–8
Charbonneau, Toussaint, 4–6, 20,
    24, 45, 51–52, 77, 108

arrogance of, 18–19
failings of, 24–26, 39, 53, 105
and Sacagawea's illness, 34–35
in St. Louis, 107
and son (Pomp), 16, 92
Chinookan Indians, 68–69, 85–88
Chinook Indians, 73, 75
Christmas, 11, 81
Clark, William, ix–x, 6, 20, 82–83
  Christmas gift for, 81
  flash flood incident, 39–40
  and grizzly bear, 29–30
  horse trading, 51–53
  and Indians, 49, 90, 96
  map-making, 80
  and Pomp, 17, 67, 92, 101, 105,
    107–8
  return trip, 93–94, 97–102
  Rocky Mountain crossing, 58
  and Sacagawea, 28, 33–34,
    45–46, 81–82, 106
  sickness of, 77
Clatsop Indians, 75, 76, 79
Clearwater River, 61–64, 91
Columbia River, 65, 69, 71, 72–75

Cascades rapids, 68–69
Celilo Falls, 68, 76
    return trip, 85–86
Corps of Discovery, 9, 20, 66–68
    Rocky Mountain crossing, 55–58
    winter headquarters, 76–83
Crow Indians, 100
Cruzatte (Private), 11, 24–25, 32,
    64, 69, 90, 104

Dancing, 11, 32, 64, 69, 90
Dog meat, 67
Drouillard, George, 20, 29, 44, 47,
    63, 93

Elk meat, 77, 79
Ermine tails, 45, 81

Flash flood, 38–40
Flathead Indians, 56, 66, 68–69
Fleas, 69, 74, 80
Food, on journey, 23–24, 28, 59, 77,
    91, 98, 105
    Rocky Mountain crossing, 57–58
Fort Clatsop, 79–80
Fort Mandan, 8–10, 13–15, 104

Gallatin River, 43, 99
Great Falls, 37–38, 41, 97, 99
Great Medicine Day (Christmas),
    11
Grizzly bears, 27–31, 38
Gros Ventres. See Minnetaree
    Indians

Hidatsas. See Minnetaree Indians
Horse meat, 57–58

Horses, 7, 41, 51–54, 56
    stolen by Indians, 100, 101, 103

Insects, 28, 43, 101

Jefferson, Thomas (Great Father),
    ix, 5, 29, 65, 90, 104
Jefferson River, 43–44, 98
Jesseaume, René, 7, 14, 16, 104
Journey of Discovery, x–xi, 7, 106
    plans for, 14–15
Jumping Fish (girlhood friend),
    48

Lemhi Pass, 51, 53–54
Lewis, Meriwether, ix–x, 6, 14, 20,
    51, 58, 60, 80
    explorations, 97–98, 101–5
    and Indians, 96
        Shoshones, 44–50, 52
        thieving, 86–88
    return trip, 93–94
    and Sacagawea, 16, 26, 52–53
    sickness of, 34–36
    wounding of, 104
Lolo Trail, 56–58, 91, 93–96
Louisiana Territory, ix

Madison River, 43, 99
Mandan Indians, 6–7, 13, 14, 21,
    96, 104
Marias River, 33, 97, 103
Minnetaree Indians, x, 2, 4–5, 8–9,
    11, 14, 18, 21, 96, 104, 106
Missouri River, 20, 32–33, 97
Moccasins, 36, 37, 80
Mosquitoes, 28, 33, 43, 101

Nez Percé Indians, 59–61, 90–91
  as guides, 63–64, 93–96
NunumBi, 70, 76, 80, 85

Old Toby, 55–57, 60, 62–63
Otter Woman, 5, 8–10, 15, 21

Pacific Ocean, 74, 82
  route to, 6–7
Pirogues, 20, 25–26, 33, 37, 101,
  103–4, 106
Point Distress, 73–74
Pomp. See Charbonneau, Jean
  Baptiste
Pompy's Tower, 101
Prickly pear cactus, 43

Rattlesnakes, 28, 38
Rivers, names of, 32, 33, 43
Rocky Mountains, 7, 41, 55–58
  return trip, 91, 93–96

Sacagawea, ix–xi, 1–3, 8–15, 17–19,
  20, 21, 53, 65, 107
  adventures of, 25–26, 38–40
  birth of daughter, 107–8
  birth of son, 15–16
  blue-beaded belt, 75–76
  contributions of, 23–24, 38,
    60–61, 63–64, 77–78, 80,
    89–91, 105–6
  death of, 107–8
  food prejudices of, 57–58, 67
  and hostile Indians, 70 86–88
  and Pomp's illness, 91–92
  return trip, 93–96, 98–102

Rocky Mountain crossing, 55–58
  and Shoshones, 41–50, 51–53
  sickness of, 33–36
  and whale, 81–83
St. Louis, x, 5, 105, 107
Salmon, 64, 66, 69
Salt making, 80
Seaman (Lewis' dog), 13, 20, 29,
  38, 43, 74, 86, 97
Shoshone Indians, x–xi, 2, 7, 8,
  23–24, 41–47, 51–53
  prisoners, 89, 90
Sign language, 44–45, 46, 47,
  63
Snake Indians. *See* Shoshone
  Indians
Snake River, 64–65

Tetoharsky, 63, 67, 69–70, 90
Three Forks, 43, 99
Twisted Hair, 60, 61, 63–65, 67,
  69–70, 91

Walla Walla Indians, 67, 89
Wanapam Indians, 66
Wapato roots, 73–74, 75, 77
Weather, 56–57, 79–80
  rainy, 71–75, 83, 85
Whale, 81–83
Whitewater canoeing, 62–65,
  68–69
Wildlife studies, x, 19, 28–29, 80

Yelleppit, 67–68, 89–90
Yellowstone River, 32, 97, 99–100
York (servant), 11, 13, 23, 69